Access your online resources

SEND Assessment is accompanied by a number of printable online materials, designed to ensure this resource best supports your professional needs.

Activate your online resources:

Go to www.routledge.com/cw/speechmark and click on the cover of this book.

Click the 'Sign in or Request Access' button and follow the instructions in order to access the resources.

Please also visit the Willow Tree Learning website at www.willowtreelearning. co.uk for further resources and examples.

'The structured format and simple, non-jargon, language is a real strength of this book. It doesn't just focus on what the child can't do, but instead ensures the assessors are actively looking for the child's strengths too, something that can often be overlooked when a child presents with SEND. The 7 distinct areas are all linked by the letter 'C' making them memorable. The Tracker also generates a quantifiable number, so the impact of additional support can be measured.'

Nadine Avenal, SEND Lead – Sapientia Education Trust

'We are just starting to use Judith's "7 C's" and can already see that it has immense potential for tracking and measuring progress in areas that cannot be tracked using traditional methods. I think it will be very helpful in allowing us to support the child in their wider personal development and will allow for a more individualised and collaborative approach.'

Cherie Pointon, SENCO – Dell Primary

'It has been such a valuable tool to enable staff to broaden their language around the children's barriers to learning and enabled us to be specific in the support that we implement. It supports the children in understanding their barriers and ensures that they are part of the process when planning their next steps and allows them to take the ownership of their progress.'

Maria Hodges, SENCO – Millfield Primary

SEND Assessment

This invaluable resource offers practical ideas and materials to allow SENCOs and SEN practitioners to capture learning, demonstrate the impact of SEN support, and analyse whether provision is effectively tackling barriers to learning.

Chapters introduce a shared *language of learning* and move through seven key components: cognition, communication, creativity, control, compassion, co-ordination and the curriculum.

Key features include:

- A framework for the holistic assessment of skills and attributes that contribute to accessing the curriculum, and a framework for intervention that is additional to, or different from, the differentiated curriculum;
- A unique strengths-based progress tracker that establishes a baseline to inform intervention and determine progress over time;
- A photocopiable and downloadable programme of materials, trialled and tested in both primary and secondary settings, that can be shared with teachers, senior leaders and support staff, as well as with parents/carers and pupils.

Providing a framework to create a holistic profile of the child and their needs, *SEND Assessment* empowers professionals to confidently demonstrate progress for barriers to learning that are otherwise difficult to measure. It will support SENCOs in their day-to-day roles and become a vital tool for those interested in providing effective SEN provision in educational settings.

Judith Carter is a registered Educational Psychologist (EP) and Director of Willow Tree Learning. She has worked as a Senior Specialist EP (Inclusion & Autism) in Essex, Norfolk and Suffolk, and was a Senior Adviser for Inclusion & SEN-D working in school improvement within a Local Authority. It was here that she trained as an Ofsted inspector. She is a Tutor on the National Award for SEN Co-ordination working with Eastern Partnership and hosts the Essential SENCO Network and provides a range of bespoke training on SEND. Judith believes passionately in inclusion and education for all and works directly with staff, children, young people and their families, to promote participation and learning.

SEND Assessment

A Strengths-based Framework for Learners with SEND

JUDITH CARTER

Routledge
Taylor & Francis Group

LONDON AND NEW YORK

First published 2021
by Routledge
2 Park Square, Milton Park, Abingdon, Oxon OX14 4RN

and by Routledge
605 Third Avenue, New York, NY 10158

Routledge is an imprint of the Taylor & Francis Group, an informa business

British Library Cataloguing-in-Publication Data
A catalogue record for this book is available from the British Library

Library of Congress Cataloging-in-Publication Data
Names: Carter, Judith, author.
Title: SEND assessment : a strengths-based framework for learners with SEND /
Judith Carter.
Description: Abingdon, Oxon ; New York : Routledge, 2021. |
Series: The essential SENCO toolkit | Includes bibliographical references and index.
Identifiers: LCCN 2020048710 (print) | LCCN 2020048711 (ebook) |
ISBN 9780367632878 (hardback) | ISBN 9780367632861 (paperback) |
ISBN 9781003118640 (ebook)
Subjects: LCSH: Learning disabled children—Education. | Special education—Evaluation.
Classification: LCC LC4704 .C375 2021 (print) | LCC LC4704 (ebook) |
DDC 371.9—dc23
LC record available at https://lccn.loc.gov/2020048710
LC ebook record available at https://lccn.loc.gov/2020048711

ISBN: 978-0-367-63287-8 (hbk)
ISBN: 978-0-367-63286-1 (pbk)
ISBN: 978-1-003-11864-0 (ebk)

Typeset in Bembo
by codeMantra

Access the companion website: www.routledge.com/cw/speechmark

Contents

Acknowledgements

As a child in the 1980s, Captain Sensible told me "you've got to have a dream, if you don't have a dream, how you gonna have a dream come true?" (For those of you who were not children in the 1980s, Captain Sensible sang a 'pop' song called 'Happy Talk' in 1982.) And for me, writing this book is a dream come true! I would like to thank Matt Cooper, my amazing partner and best friend, who has supported me in the pursuit of this dream and my Mum and Dad, who taught me how to dream in the first place. Thank you also to my friends (especially Roo Vyas-Smith, Caj Barker, Jess Fitt, Colin and Angie Thomas), who always support and encourage me to keep going!

I would like to thank some of the inspirational colleagues that I have worked with over the years in Essex, Norfolk and Suffolk including Jo Lyons, Andre Imich, Allan Sigston, Sue Kerfoot, Jean Law, the incredible 'cutting edge' original Assistant EP cohort: Jacqui Horan, Catherine Court, Liz Norman, Claire Counsell and Helen Peters. As well as Simon Claridge, Fiona Ayres, Sydney Bayley, Ros Somerville, Caryl Carr, Helen Phelan, Terry Cook, Lisa Christensen, Claire Darwin, Elaine Price (and the entire Northern team), Marie Osborne, Emma Walton, Rachel Wilson, Sarah Gentle, Becky Dixon, Jo Hodges and Angela Scott. As well as Tony Booth and Artemi Sakellariadis, who both inspired and encouraged my self-efficacy. Thank you also to DNEAT, St Benet's Multi Academy Trust and the Sapienta Education Trust, whose staff and SENCOs have supported the development of this work, particularly Nadine Avenal, Rachael Judd and Simon Morely. And of course, to Jean Gross, who is simply a 'jeanius', not to mention Lev Vygotsky, who underpins my professional thinking and practice.

The book is however dedicated to the incredible SENCOs I work directly with and those within the Essential SENCO Network hosted in Norfolk and the brilliant children, young people, families, staff and governors in our schools. It is a privilege to know and work with so many of you, and I thank you for your dedication, commitment, resilience and humanity. You inspire me every day!

Finally thank you to Little Miss Sunshine (aka Sunni), our Yorkie-poo puppy, who has reminded me that however busy I think I am, there is always time to throw a squeaky ball!

Introduction

Welcome to *SEND Assessment: A Strengths-based Framework for Learners with SEND*.
I am far more familiar with being a reader of books rather than an author, but as a
reader and user of books, I have a relevant insight into what I look for in a book:
I value practical information presented in an accessible and enjoyable manner. My
favourite books promote thinking and motivate me to 'have a go' at something new.
They also give me confidence and inspire me to keep going on what, at times, can
feel like a lonely professional journey. I hope that this book fulfils your aspirations
and I assure you, I will do my best to ensure that it does not disappoint!

This is the first of a series of practical books called *The Essential SENCO Toolkit*
and, as the name suggests, the books have been written to support SENCOs and
SEN Practitioners in fulfilling their professional duties. In essence the book has been
written for *you* and, has been inspired by the many dedicated and brilliant SENCO
colleagues that I have worked with and continue to work with. The purpose of
the book is to provide a starting-point of practical ideas and resources. However,
as with every idea, please use it to add to your own thinking. The resources are
photocopiable, but do adapt them to suit your individual learners and your learning
context. Materials can also be downloaded via the Routledge Speechmark weblink,
details of which are at the front of the book. Many of the ideas are biased towards
supporting learners with SEN in mainstream primary and secondary, but with your
skill and imagination you could adapt the ideas to suit learning in a nursery, college,
special or independent setting. The only request is that you share your adaptations
and thoughts, so that as a profession, we continue to operate collaboratively to
promote our shared 'best endeavours', leading to the highest quality provision and
outcomes for **all** learners.

The book has been written to be read in full or to be dipped into. I am privileged
to own a vast array of books; some I hugely value but have never actually read
from cover to cover! Instead, I have gained an overview of the book and extracted
chunks that made the most sense to me at the time. Over the years I return to the
books and often add new chunks to those that have become an integral part of my
work. So, however you choose to read this, the resources are designed to support
and develop your thinking. It is important to stress that the intention of this book
is to provide a 'practical' starting-point, so of course the theory underpinning the
approach and suggestions are discussed, but this is not a theoretical text. There are

some tremendous texts and websites that explore the theories referred to in far more detail and if this is an area of interest to you, or you are completing action research such as required in the National Award in SEN Co-ordination, I would certainly encourage you to research this further. The references will aid your exploration, but the decision has been taken to retain a practical 'lens' throughout this book.

For over 25 years I have been privileged to work in education. I have been a Primary Teacher, Senior Educational Psychologist, an LA Senior Adviser SEN-D, Ofsted Inspector, SEN-D Trainer and Consultant and I am also a Tutor with Eastern Partnership, who deliver the National Award in SEN Co-ordination. I now work for Willow Tree Learning, which is my own company, offering bespoke Educational Psychology, SEND training and inclusive school improvement services. In every role, my priority was promoting education for *all* children and young people. In recent years this was achieved by direct work with staff, particularly SENCOs and SEN Practitioners. I host the 'Essential SENCO Network' in Norfolk and noticed that colleagues shared a passion and commitment to improve learning for all pupils and welcomed ideas and exemplars to support the development of their practice. This inspired me to create a starting-point for them, and on many occasions, with them. It is these 'starting-points' that are presented across the *Essential SENCO Toolkit* mini-series, starting with *SEND Assessment*. If you like the content of this book and wish to exchange and explore ideas with others, please consider joining our Essential SENCO Forum (at no charge,) which is available at www. willowtreelearning.co.uk or join the Essential SENCO Network and attend our 'virtual' termly meetings.

1. What is assessment?

Assessment is at the heart of education. It is an essential component of learning focused teaching and it dominates a huge part of our everyday lives. But how often do we consider what assessment *actually is* and whether this meaning is the same for the teacher and the learner?

The Cambridge English Dictionary defines assessment as: 'the act of judging or deciding the amount, value, quality, or importance of something, or the judgement or decision that is made'. It continues, saying that assessment is: 'the process of considering all the information about a situation or a person and making a judgement'.

It is often quite 'humbling' to reflect on the definition of words that have become such an integral part of our vocabulary. How poignant to be reminded that the word and indeed process involves 'judgement' and by implication 'value'. So often our assessments for learners with special educational needs become negative judgements as we are evaluating difficulties or barriers. Of course, our intention is to inform positive action that will support development, but it is essential that we recognise the 'deficit' model of which we are a part.

On the subject of deficit models, it is important to acknowledge that the very title of this book, the key abbreviation that we will be using throughout this text (SEN) and indeed many of our job titles, have been created as part of a deficit or medical model. If you are not yet familiar with the medical and social model of disability, I encourage you to read up on this as it reminds us of the bias that exists within us and is all around us. The medical model attributes responsibility for the disability to the individual; it is 'their' issue, whereas the social model of disability attributes the barriers experienced to the shared social environment. It acknowledges that an impairment is experienced by an individual, but the impairment becomes disabling because of limitations within the social environment. An example cited by the University of Leicester is that of a wheelchair user who is unable to get into a building because there are only steps. The medical model attributes this barrier to the *wheelchair* (and by implication the wheelchair user). In contrast the social model attributes the barrier to the *steps* (and by implication the building owners and designers). At first glance this may appear to be somewhat trivial or pedantic, but in real terms, the significance of attribution cannot be overstated as it relates to 'ownership' and responsibility. The medical model attributes all responsibility to the individual so it is *their* responsibility to overcome or remove barriers they face.

Whereas the social model is more inclusive and perceives that the responsibility is with the society and the environment, which are external to the individual, so there is a shared need to overcome or remove the barriers.

The term 'special educational needs' or SEN evolved from what some now consider to be a controversial history of the educational language of 'difference'. The introduction of the term 'special educational needs' emerged within the Warnock Report published in 1978. This report (in)famously cited that 20 per cent of children could at some point have a special educational need. It is unclear whether this was a statement of accuracy or a self-fulfilling prophecy. But either way, for many years, the assumption remained that 20 per cent of children had SEN. The Education Act 1981 assimilated the term SEN and allocated responsibility to the then Local Education Authorities to identify and assess children who might have a special need, in order to offer appropriate provision, a system which, although it has witnessed three versions of a Code of Practice (soon to be four,) has largely remained the same. The first Code of Practice for identifying SEN was published in 1994. This created a five-stage process of identification, including the introduction of a Statement of SEN. The second Code, published following the SEN and Disability Act 2001, was deemed more progressive as it sought to replace the perceived 'hierarchy' associated with the five-stage model and introduced the framework of 'School/Early Years action' and 'School/Early Years action plus'. The third Code was described at its launch in 2014 as the most 'radical change' in the SEN system for 30 years. It established a single category of SEN Support and introduced the Education, Health and Care Plan which replaced the Statement of SEN. At the time of writing, this Code is under review, with revisions expected in the future.

The intention of the introduction of the term SEN was undoubtedly positive. The Warnock committee at the time were attempting to move away from the negative and utterly reductionist terms of the 11 categories of 'handicap' established with the 1944 Education Act, including 'educationally subnormal, imbecile and delicate'. Within that context, the term 'special' can be considered as an attempt to move towards a more positive language intended to promote value. However, ironically for many, the longevity of this term has in fact created a distinction or separation between groups of children and young people instead of uniting them.

In reality, every child is special and unique and should be valued. Yet the language of SEN in many ways continues to focus on negative difference rather than similarity. The term also created a construct of difference, which implied the need for additional expertise or 'specialist' knowledge. In fact, **inclusive education is not 'specialist' or delivered by 'experts' but it is simply personal, flexible and bespoke. The process of learning itself, if stripped back, is the same, but the presentation, rate and mode of delivery is tailored and personalised.** Tony Booth and Mel Ainscow, within the Index for Inclusion (2011), state that 'inclusion is about increasing participation for all children and adults. It is about supporting schools to become more responsive to the diversity of children's backgrounds, interests, experience, knowledge and skills.' If we could remove the word 'special' from SEN, we would be referring to 'educational needs' which by definition is inclusive as we all have individual educational needs! What is more, the professional group who are trained and skilled to meet educational needs is, of course, us! Teachers would be empowered to meet educational needs, rather than risk feeling 'unskilled' by the construct of needing to deliver 'special' educational needs.

We do, however, live and work in a system that has embedded this term at its heart and many parents and carers advocate for the term special educational needs, because after all, to every parent or carer their child is special. We are also working in an imperfect system which is often not inclusive; as such, parents and carers seek 'protection' for their child. So over four decades since its introduction, we continue to refer to SEN and indeed the very job title of a SENCO reinforces this construct. Of course, as one practitioner it would be very difficult to simply 'drop' the word 'special' from SEN, as it would be very difficult to write a SENCO toolkit that does not include the abbreviation SEN, but let us at least use our language mindfully. Knowing the origins and, at times, pitfalls of the very language of our system can help us to reduce the risk of negative implications. It also promotes thinking and conversation within our profession, which can only further support our progression. Only time will tell, if our future colleagues will feel shame and disappointment when they read the abbreviation SEN, in the same way as I feel shame and disappointment when I read the term 'imbecile' and 'educationally subnormal'. But for now, let's get back to assessment.

> In education, the term **assessment** refers to the wide variety of methods or tools that educators use to evaluate, measure, and document the academic readiness, learning progress, skill acquisition, or educational needs of students.
>
> (The Glossary of Education Reform, 2015)

This immediately feels more 'familiar' and reminds us of the many and varied activities that we undertake to 'assess, plan, do and review' the learning needs of those children and young people identified with SEN. Ironically, it is such an essential part of our work that we do not always notice the varied assessment tasks we undertake. Of course, we are aware of the formal assessment activities, especially when the results of these activities are used directly or indirectly to inform the assessment of our own professional activities. But there are of course, many different forms of assessment, some of which will be explored here.

Formative and summative assessment are the dominant assessment types used in education. Formative assessment, as the name suggests, relates to gathering information to *inform* action. Paul Black and Dylan William in 1998 assimilated the findings of research into assessment in their crucial text *Inside the Black Box*. This work was, and still is, highly influential in linking formative assessment, known as 'assessment for learning' to raising standards and attainment. If you are not familiar with the *Black Box* series, I would highly recommend this to you, as it remains challenging and thought-provoking two decades after original publication. Black and William define assessment as follows:

> …the term 'assessment' refers to all those activities undertaken by teachers, *and by their students in assessing themselves*, which provide information to be used as feedback to modify the teaching and learning activities in which they are engaged. *Such assessment becomes 'formative assessment' when the evidence is actually used to adapt the teaching work to meet the needs.*
>
> (Black and William, 1998, page 2)

Here the emphasis is on the *use* and potential application of the information gathered, which defines the assessment as formative. In contrast, summative assessment provides a summary of attainment, skills or knowledge gathered at a specific point in time.

Black and William became huge advocates for formative assessment as their analysis of the research concluded that 'assessment for learning' was highly influential in improving learning and raising standards. They also promoted the role of student 'self-evaluation' and teacher –student dialogue within formative assessment, stating that:

> For formative assessment to be productive, pupils should be trained in self-assessment so that they can understand the main purposes of their learning and thereby grasp what they need to do to achieve.
>
> (Black and William, 1998, page 10)

This description of pupil self-assessment as 'an essential component of formative assessment' (page 10) and not just a luxury, underpins the SEN assessment framework to be presented in this book. It also fits alongside the principles of strength-based assessment which will be explored in the next chapter, as self-assessment seeks to promote the identification of strengths and areas for development as an essential aspect of future learning. Black and William also promoted the contribution of dialogue between the teacher and pupil, saying that:

> Dialogue with the teacher provides the opportunity for the teacher to respond to and re-orient the pupil's thinking.

(page 11)

They also acknowledged the risk that a teacher may inadvertently inhibit future learning for pupils by their unconscious responses – the implication being that teachers will impact on learning, either positively or negatively, so of course, for leaders including SENCOs and SEN Practitioners, it is essential to ensure that the impact of teachers is positive. This has huge ramifications for professional practice with learners with SEND. After all, this group of learners are often assessed even more than others! They engage in curriculum attainment assessment and then often undergo additional tasks with the SENCO and or SEN practitioner, who may then seek further assessment from outside agencies. **But is there a risk that 'our' SEN focused assessment is more about summative information than formative information? If the definition of formative assessment is explicitly linked with the application of the impact on teaching, are we sure that our SEN assessment information actually filters back and influences teaching? Or despite our best efforts to achieve this, does SEN assessment simply generate information that is an 'add-on' and does not directly influence the quality of teaching received by the learner?**

Educationalists have a vast array of assessment *tools* that they can use to carry out both formative and summative assessments. These include standardised or psychometric tests which measure specific aspects of *what* a child has learnt, so can be considered as having more of a summative purpose. In comparison, dynamic or interactive assessment tasks can be used to explore *how* a child is learning, which is more formative in purpose as the information can be used to inform the shared learning experience of the child and teacher at that moment. In addition, there are curriculum-based assessments, which compare performance against the curricular objectives and play-based assessments which explore skills and knowledge during play.

The assessment tools described above can be applied into various assessment *activities* which tend to offer either norm-referenced, criterion-referenced or ipsative information. Norm-referenced assessment compares performance to an expectation or a national 'norm'. Criterion-referenced compares against a specific requirement or goal. Ipsative assessments can be used to compare a pupil's performance with their prior performance but no comparison to others is made. There are also diagnostic assessments that seek to identify strengths and difficulties or prior knowledge and skills and whether this information indicates a specific diagnosis. Of course, in reality very little is as simple as that sounds! Summative tasks can be used formatively, just as standardised tests can be used to facilitate dynamic or interactive tasks. But, at the time of use, are we aware of the purpose and intended contribution of the information we collect and do our pupils have the same view?

As educationalists we adapt our resources and approach and very rarely adopt such 'clinical' and discreet application of concepts, (unless it is a requirement for a research project). Instead we adopt an eclectic approach and develop our own preferred practices which for the majority serve us well. However, **this can lead to a less mindful approach to assessment, where there is a risk that we 'sleep-walk' into the use of deficit language or we take short-cuts by talking about children and young people as percentile scores or standardised test results, which reinforces the bias of a 'can't do' approach, as opposed to describing what they 'can do' with and without help.** Perhaps you have heard a teacher or indeed yourself, refer to a child as being the '4th percentile' instead of detailing their learning profile? There is no intent to blame or shame you by describing this, indeed quite the contrary. You are encouraged to notice this about your own practice or should that say, *we* are encouraged to notice this about *our* own practice (as I too have to guard against this risk in my work), so that we can offer a greater insight and information about a child or young person, that will help others to develop the most effective learning opportunities for that pupil.

The narrative of assessment is often presented from the perspective of the educationalist, as our selection of tools or approaches is influenced by the expected information we will gain from the activity. The text you have read illustrates this perfectly. The description of the types and range of assessment tools was all from the view of an 'assessor'. What will you gain from each approach? How will you use and apply this information? The rationale for this is that you can use the information gained to inform actions that will ultimately improve access to learning for the child or young person. **But what if the assessment itself could be part of a process that improved access to learning for the child or young person? What if**

the shared assessment experience *became* **part of their learning?** Instead of selecting assessment tasks that give us information, what if we opted for an assessment experience that was a collaboration and provided the learner with an insight into their strengths as well as their next steps for action? This is the exact intention of adopting a strengths-based approach to assessment, whereby the process itself gives an insight into what tools or skills the learner is already 'bringing to the table', the identification of which can be used to utilise and aid future learning. Details of this approach will be explored in Chapter 2.

Implications for SENCOs and SEN Practitioners

Assessment is of course a fundamental part of your role, yet I wonder how often we evaluate the rationale and origins of our assessment activities? Is it more likely that we adopt the approach and tools that we inherit from our predecessors or we choose to buy assessment tests or tools that we think will be useful without necessarily considering the type of assessment activity we will be creating? Yet the advantage of such analysis is greater insight into the type of information we are gathering and its subsequent advantages and limitations. So, what does each approach offer a SENCO or SEN practitioner and ultimately the learner?

Formative and summative

Both formative and summative approaches to assessment are useful for SENCOs and SEN Practitioners. You can gather information that builds on the information already collated by teachers and parents/carers. Formative approaches can help to plan action and to predict responses to support, but ultimately should influence how teaching is planned and delivered. Similarly, summative assessment can demonstrate acquired knowledge or the assimilation of taught information. In real terms you may use observation, mediation, questioning, scaffolding, work scrutiny and practical apparatus to aid formative assessment. You may use tests, quizzes, exams and responses to specific tasks to gather summative information. You are most likely to use a combination of approaches.

Psychometric and Dynamic Assessment

I am a huge advocate of Dynamic Assessment both within my own work but in particular for application by teachers, SENCOs and SEN Practitioners. Fraser

Lauchlan and Donna Carrigan, in their superb book *Improving Learning through Dynamic Assessment : A Practical Classroom Resource* detail the potential of using and describe details for applying Dynamic Assessment for teachers. They skilfully adapt Feuerstein's cognitive functions to identify learning principles and provide excellent resources for the teacher and child to baseline skills as well as providing practical action that staff and parents/carers can then use to develop these skills. The book also summarises the origins of Dynamic Assessment, which is Vygotskian in nature. Lev Vygotsky was a Russian psychologist and educator who was born in 1896, the same year as Jean Piaget. He graduated from Moscow University in 1917 and taught literature and psychology for 7 years. Vygotsky wrote over 100 books before his death at the age of 37, yet very few of them were published. His work was also banned in Russia following the Revolution and political changes at that time. His work was only translated into English in the 1960s, by which time the theories of others (including Piaget) were well embedded. Yet his social learning theory and constructs such as the zone of proximal development were and remain highly influential in education. (The zone of proximal development is the point where a learner is transitioning from what they know, to learning something new. I am often aware of when I am 'in' my own zone of proximal development as I often start to get a headache – as I *nearly* get something, but I'm not quite there yet! As educators, it is the greatest privilege to observe and even better, to have facilitated the zone of proximal development in a learner, as you are literally observing 'learning' taking place.) Vygotsky's social learning theory underpins Dynamic Assessment. Reuben Feuerstein (1921–2014), who was an Israeli clinical, developmental and cognitive psychologist, is often considered to be one of the 'founders' of Dynamic Assessment. It was his work with Moroccan, Jewish and Berber children in the 1950s that led to the original concept of 'learning potential' and the 'mediated learning experience' (MLE). Feuerstein questioned the validity of the concept of intelligence being 'fixed' and static, promoting instead the concept of cognitive modifiability. His own work with learners found that those who had been considered to be of low intelligence were able to do far more than they 'should' have been able to according to the prior assessment. Feuerstein identified what were then called 'deficient cognitive functions' and established tools for evaluation which became known as the Learning Propensity Assessment Device (LPAD.) He established instrumental enrichment programmes to develop cognitive functions and build meta-cognition with learners.

Over the years, Dynamic Assessment has grown and developed a significant following, resulting in the development of many identified 'tools' and approaches. Colleagues including David Tzuriel and Ruth Deutsch have advanced understanding around Dynamic Assessment and further developed tools for assessment. Ruth Deutsch and Michelle G. Mohammed created the Cognitive Abilities Profile (CAP), which is an incredibly powerful tool used by psychologists and teachers to identify the cognitive profile of learners, the purpose being to help focus the development of teaching that will maximise learning potential.

In essence, the opportunity for SENCOs and SEN Practitioners, is that by facilitating a 'mediated learning experience' with a child, this may help to reveal how the child is learning and how they respond to intervention or mediation. Yes of course you can use the CAP or the Complex Figure Drawing Task (developed by Rey, 1956) or any other identified DA tool, but actually as long as you adhere to the components of Dynamic Assessment you can use any stimulus. An activity becomes a dynamic assessment task through the intended creation of a mediated learning experience. Deutsch and Mohammad identify three universal criteria of MLE. These are:

1. **Intentionality** of the adult to use the interaction to foster or develop a cognitive change and **reciprocity**, shared communication with the learner of the cognitive goals of the task or situation: What are we going to learn?

2. **Communication** of meaning and purpose: Why is this useful and important?

3. **Deliberate transfer and generalisation** from the immediate experience to other applications – transcendence: Where else can we use this skill?

(Deutsch and Mohammad, 2010)

These principles underpin the strengths-based approach to assessment presented in this book and have influenced the development of the 7 Cs Learning Portfolio outlined in Chapters 5, 6 and 7.

Curriculum and play-based assessment

Curriculum and play-based assessment activities are undoubtedly what informs a significant part of our information gathering for learners in schools and settings. Often, we observe or assess learners as they complete specific curriculum tasks or we observe them at play, using and manipulating a range of toys or activities as well as engaging with or alongside others. All of these tasks give us information, but each approach tends to focus on one aspect of the learning process and or the learner, rather than the learner as a whole. We apply norm-referencing or criterion referencing to 'judge' if a skill or task has been achieved. We may use ipsative referencing to evidence-base progress from what the learner could initially do and what they can now do. However, generally our conclusions are informed by the difficulty or 'deficit' with little or no attention to strengths. For our learners with SEND it is likely that all of their assessments form a 'list' or a description of what they 'can't do' rather than anything they can. Developing a strengths-based approach to assessment can help to bring 'balance' to our descriptions as well as empower and inform the learner themselves about the tools for learning they do have.

To encourage your conscious evaluation of tasks, tools and activities, you may find it useful to develop an 'assessment index' for staff. This resource, when completed, can present the range of assessment 'options' or tools available in your school or setting and can provide an overview for application. You can collate resources into a single index (like the example that follows) or create an index for each category of need (as shown in the templates.) It may be interesting to monitor the tools and approaches that are used most often and compare these against the needs or barriers to learning identified. For example, if you have a high number of learners identified with social, emotional and mental health needs, but the most frequently used assessment is a reading test, you may want to discuss this. As with all of the tools presented here, they are offered as a possible starting point, so please consider whether this could be useful to you and if so do you need to adapt it to make the most sense in your setting? If yes, trust yourself and have a go!

Example Assessment Index

Assessment Tool or Activity	Category of Need	What Is it?	Why Use It?	With Whom?	How Often?	Anticipated Impact?	Actual Impact?
British Picture Vocabulary Scale (BPVS)	Communication & Interaction	A standardised test of receptive vocabulary (understanding)	Indicates the learners understanding of single words	Age 4+	Baseline and review maximum 6 monthly.	Provides information to adults regarding the learners understanding of spoken words.	
Phonological Assessment Battery (PhAB 2)	Cognition & Learning	Various activities that explore a range of phonological awareness skills.	To baseline phonological skills.	Age 5 years – 11 years	Baseline and review over time.	Identification of specific skills or gaps to inform planning and support.	
Strengths & Weaknesses Questionnaire (SDQ)	Social, Emotional & Mental Health	This is a self-report screening tool.	To baseline perceived strengths & weaknesses	Age 2 years – 17 years	Baseline and review to capture changes	Helps to identify perceived strengths and difficulties, aids planning.	
Working Memory Rating Scale	Cognition & Learning	A behavioural rating scale for teachers to help identify working memory capacity.	To inform teacher of pupil working memory capacity.	Age 5 years – 11 years	Baseline and review over time.	Process of completing the scale will help inform teacher of range of working memory capacity.	
Movement Assessment Battery for Children	Physical &/or Sensory	Provides an evaluation of motor skills and helps to identify areas for development.	To create a baseline of motor skills.	Age 3 – 16 years 11 months	Baseline and review over time.	Establishes a starting- point and informs the areas for development.	

Assessment Index
Cognition and Learning

Assessment Tool or Activity	What Is It?	Why Use It?	With Whom?	How Often?	Anticipated Impact?	Actual Impact?

Assessment Index
Communication and Interaction

Assessment Tool or Activity	What Is It?	Why Use It?	With Whom?	How Often?	Anticipated Impact?	Actual Impact?

Assessment Index
Social, Emotional and Mental Health

Assessment Tool or Activity	What Is It?	Why Use It?	With Whom?	How Often?	Anticipated Impact?	Actual Impact?

Assessment Index
Physical and Sensory

Assessment Tool or Activity	What Is It?	Why Use It?	With Whom?	How Often?	Anticipated Impact?	Actual Impact?

Reflections...

- Within your role, what types of assessments do you tend to use the most?
- What *happens* to the assessment information you gather as a SENCO or SEN Practitioner?
- Are learners involved in the assessment *process* or do they simply complete the assessment *product*?

References

Cambridge English Dictionary (2020). 'Assessment'. Available at https://dictionary.cambridge.org/dictionary/english/assessment (Accessed 13 September 2020).

Code of Practice on the Identification and Assessment of Special Educational Needs (1994). Department for Education.

Cognitive Abilities Profile – Administration and Scoring Manual (2010). Ruth M. Deutsch & Michelle G. Mohammed. Canterbury: Real Press. www.realpress.co.uk

Complex Figure Drawing Test (1956) Rey. Available at https://faculty.biu.ac.il/~tzuried/complex_figure_test.html (Accessed on 13 September 2020)

Dynamic Assessment: From Theory to Practice (2015) Mohammad Saber Khaghaninejad. LAP Lambert Academic Publishing.

Education Act (1944). Available at https://www.legislation.gov.uk/ukpga/Geo6/7-8/31/contents (Accessed on 13 September 2020)

Improving Learning through Dynamic Assessment – A Practical Classroom Resource (2013) Fraser Lauchlan and Donna Carrigan. London: Jessica Kingsley Publishers.

Index for Inclusion: Developing Learning and Participation in Schools (2011). Tony Booth and Mel Ainscow. Bristol: Centre for Studies in Inclusive Education (CSIE).

Inside the Black Box: Raising Standards through Classroom Assessment (1998). Paul Black and Dylan William. Brentford, London: GL Assessment.

Special Educational Needs and Disability Code of Practice: 0 to 25 years – Statutory Guidance for Organisations which Work with and Support Children and Young People who have Special Educational Needs or Disabilities (2014; updated 2015). Department for Education and Department of Health.

Special Educational Needs Code of Practice (2001). Department for Education and Skills.

The Dynamic Assessment of Retarded Performers: The Learning Potential Assessment Device, Theory, Instruments and Techniques (1979) Feuerstein, Rand & Hoffman. Baltimore, MD: University Park Press.

The Glossary of Education Reform (2015). Available at https://www.edglossary.org/assessment/ (Accessed 13 September 2020).

The Social and Medical Model of Disability (2020). Available at https://www2.le.ac.uk/offices/accessability/staff/accessabilitytutors/information-for-accessability-tutors/the-social-and-medical-model-of-disability (Accessed 13 September 2020).

The Warnock Report (1978). Available at http://www.educationengland.org.uk/documents/warnock/warnock1978.html (Accessed 13 September 2020).

2. A strengths-based approach

Adopting a strengths-based approach to assessment in many ways shifts the very purpose of assessment, from merely providing information **to** the 'assessor' (teacher), to sharing positive information **with** the 'assessed' (learner). Not only does this have the potential to boost their confidence and self-esteem, but it also provides meaningful information about the skills that they have and could attempt to apply to aid future learning. Take a moment to reflect on how often you and colleagues actively consider assessment from the learner's perspective? Of course, we engage with learners during the assessment task but are they aware of the activity or its purpose? Do they benefit from the 'process' itself or simply from the 'product' of the assessment? (The 'product' being defined as the application of the information from the teacher.) **Dare to imagine, what would it be like if the learner continued to gain from the 'product' of assessment, but also gained from the 'process'?**

In many ways, this approach builds upon the construct of the assessment activity itself, being part of a 'mediated learning experience.' The activity has intentionality as its purpose is to develop cognitive change. It also has reciprocity and shared communication, which includes a description as to why this is useful and important. It also seeks to deliberately transfer and generalise skills beyond the context of the assessment as the identified strengths can be applied in other situations. Adopting a strengths-based approach to assessment shifts the intention from simply extracting information from a learner, to sharing information *with* a learner. The role is to 'notice and discuss' rather than to 'test and return' the learner to their previous task. It perceives assessment tasks as a direct and purposeful opportunity for the learner, rather than generating information which should have an indirect benefit to the learner. (Assuming the assessor uses the information to make adaptations that ultimately promote greater participation for the learner.)

Strengths-based approaches have clear links with person-centred approaches which originate from the strand of humanistic psychology. It is reported that in the 1940s a number of psychologists, including Carl Rogers, were dissatisfied by the psychological perspectives used in counselling at the time and they sought to shift the focus on to understanding and improving the quality of the life experiences and relationships of clients. This led to the 'birth' of client-centred therapy (Rogers 1955) which further evolved into person-centred therapy and later, person-centred approaches inspired by person-centred planning.

> The phrase 'Person Centred Planning' was coined in North America in the mid-1980s to distinguish the person centred way of doing planning from so called 'service centred' approaches to planning that are solely framed by whatever services are typically available.
>
> (Newton, Wilson and Darwin, 2016, page 9)

The inclusion of person-centred approaches in the SEND Code of Practice 2014 raised its profile amongst SENCOs and SEN Practitioners. Prior to this it was an embedded approach often used within social care. There are five key features of a person-centred approach. The first is that ultimately, the person is at the centre. The approach is rooted in the principles of shared power and self- determination. The second is that family members and friends of the person are partners in planning. This approach seeks to view the person in the context of their family and community. Third, a person- centred approach seeks to reflect what is important to the person, their capacities and what support they require. It identifies capacities rather than deficits, defining what a person can do, their gifts and who they are, rather than simply listing difficulties. The fourth key feature relates to perceived relevance. Any plan should result in actions that are about the person's life and not simply a list of services that may or may not be available. The fifth key feature is that the plan is the start of a process of listening, learning and future action, as opposed to simply being a one- off event.

The adoption of this approach as a key principle within the Code of Practice 2014 had incredible potential to change the culture of schools, settings and services. Ironically however, the aspect of the approach that appears to have had the greatest impact on education practices has been the 'one-page profile'. Many schools and settings began generating one-page profiles and some were even seen as the replacement to the individual education plan (IEP.) This is ironic, as in some cases the one-page profile had the least impact on the learner, as although it was diligently completed, it was then placed in an A4 folder and referred to at review meetings! In this regard, the one- page profile really was like the IEP, which had a history of being 'generated' but not actually used to inform teaching. However, in some ways, generating a one-page profile but not using it to influence practice is worse than not writing one at all. This is because the process of creating a one-page profile involves asking the learner to identify what they are good at, what other people think they are good at and what might help them with their learning. If this is recorded and then 'ignored', the implicit message given to the learner is that that even when they express their view, no-one listens to it and it makes no difference! This commentary is not intended to 'blame' SENCOs, SEN Practitioners or teachers if they create a one-page profile with a learner but find it difficult to actually use it, but rather to encourage them to reconsider why they created it in the first place? **We should never just generate paperwork for the sake of it. There should be a clear purpose and function for the paperwork and ultimately, if it is going to have a positive impact on a learner, the learner needs to know about it and must be directly involved in its creation.** This is at the heart of the person-centred approach: doing something *with* someone, rather than doing something *to* them. And the 'something' has direct and explicit meaning and relevance to them.

A strengths-based approach seeks to identify and utilise strengths that already exist. This is particularly relevant for learners with SEND, as the very identification of them as having SEN promotes a deficit perspective of them. It is essential that we seek to promote balance, identifying strengths and barriers to learning. It is also essential that all parents/carers hear that their child has strengths and most importantly that every child hears and can identify that they have strengths. It is essential that as professionals working with children and young people and their families that we remain mindful of the language we use to describe needs. Avoid describing a learner as an 'SEN child', and although 'a child with SEN' is better, the most accurate description is to describe them by their name. By all means refer to 'Judith's learning profile' and describe her strengths and barriers to learning or areas for development, but under no circumstances describe her as 'SEN Judith'.

The strengths-based approach (just like person-centred planning), has its origins in social work. It promotes the identification of strengths as the key to enabling 'clients' to affect change for themselves. This has overlaps with motivational interviewing and solution-focused brief therapy which both further reinforce the evidence base for this way of working, but also help to provide 'tools' for application.

Motivational interviewing seeks to promote self-determined change through conversation. Instead of seeking to reward, pressure or coerce learners to change, motivational interviewing seeks to empower the learner to feel motivated to change for themselves. Rollnick, Kaplan and Rutschman (2016), in their brilliant book

Motivational Interviewing in Schools: Conversations to Improve Behaviour and Learning state:

> Motivational interviewing is not a behaviour change technique, trick or strategy done on or to students, but rather something done with them or on their behalf. It's certainly not a way of getting someone to do something he or she would not otherwise want to do. It's best not viewed as a behaviour management technique but as a way of helping someone make decisions.

Within motivational interviewing the facilitator seeks to implement four conversational patterns in an attempt to facilitate change. These are: engaging, focusing, evoking and planning. The essence of this approach and indeed person-centred planning, is that conversation 'with' someone is more powerful than any words spoken 'at' someone.

Of further relevance to a strengths-based approach is the theoretical framework of Solution Focused Therapy (also known as Solution Focused Brief Therapy.) This was developed in the 1970s by Steve de Shazer and Insoo Kim Berg and other colleagues working at Milwaukee Brief Family Therapy Center. The therapy seeks to help clients achieve positive change by identifying solutions rather than remaining focused on problems. It is a future-orientated approach that seeks to empower the person to identify an alternative version of their situation without the 'problem'. They are asked to identify 'exceptions' (times when this issue does not occur) and to identify their 'best hope' for an outcome. Solution-focused approaches have been integrated into work in education by anyone who has used a rating scale with a learner or asked a learner to set a goal. The 'miracle' question originates from this approach too and is often used to encourage children to explore best hopes.

Implications for SENCOs and SEN Practitioners

Adopting a strengths-based approach to assessment seeks to bring 'balance' to an otherwise 'deficit' model. Barriers to learning are of course identified, but alongside existing strengths. For the learner this is incredibly powerful, as instead of simply discussing difficulties and challenges, there is an opportunity to celebrate success and skills. Many SENCOs and SEN Practitioners work hard to promote the positives, referring to small-stepped progress, but the narrative often still relates to progress in overcoming difficulties rather than a celebration of strengths in their own right. It may be that the strengths are not often visible in school, particularly if a learner is an excellent gamer or always wins at chess or Cluedo, but this is even more reason to promote a dialogue about these strengths and to encourage the learner to consider if any of these skills are transferable to the areas of difficulty.

The ultimate 'power' of a strengths-based approach to assessment relates to the 'mirror' that we use to reflect information to the child. Back in 1902 a sociologist named Charles Horton Cooley first cited the 'looking-glass theory of self' (Baumeister, 1999). This evolved into symbolic interactionism, which is a perspective that seeks to understand and define the process of interaction in human behaviour. The looking-glass theory states that children develop their own sense of self from the information that is 'reflected' back to them, or at least their perception of the information that is reflected to them. Initially this is from caregivers in their family and of course then from significant adults and peers around them, including at school. **It is essential that we consider the direct and indirect messages we give to learners with SEND; for example, if we are only talking about their 'difficulties,' they will perceive that they only have difficulties. If we tell them that they 'have' to work with an adult at all times, they will perceive that they need help with everything.** Symbolic interactionism is in many ways an argument to completely 'deconstruct' the system of SEND, as it reinforces the deficit perspective itself. We as individuals may struggle to do that, but **we can mindfully seek to promote greater balance to the messages we reflect to children, young people and their families.** The promotion of a strengths-based dialogue with learners enables us to celebrate the unique and wonderfully diverse nature of every learner, whilst identifying and supporting the development of areas of need.

Reflections…

- Do you currently have a system for identifying and capturing learner strengths?
- Are learners encouraged to identify what they think they are good at?
- Do you and colleagues identify *your* strengths and seek to apply these to areas of development?

References

Client-Centred Therapy (1955) Carl Rogers. Boston: Houghton-Mifflin.

Counselling Children: A Practical Introduction (2002) Kathryn Geldard & David Geldard. London: Sage Publications.

Motivational Interviewing in Schools: Conversations to Improve Behaviour and Learning (2016) Stephen Rollnick, Sebastian G Kaplan & Richard Rutschman. New York: The Guilford Press.

Person Centred Planning Together: A Resource to Develop your Person Centred Planning Skills (2016) Colin Newton, Derek Wilson and Claire Darwin. Ipswich: Schools' Choice (Vertas).

The Self in Social Psychology (1999) Edited by Roy F. Baumeister. Philadelphia, PA: Psychology Press (Taylor & Francis).

Solution- Focused Therapy (1998) Bill O'Connell. London: Sage Publications.

3. Who has SEN, SEND and/or medical needs?

An ongoing challenge for SENCOs and SEN Practitioners is the identification of those learners with SEN, those who are Disabled and those with medical needs. It sounds obvious, but in fact, it remains one of the most talked about issues for SENCOs. **How to distinguish between a learner with SEN or a learner who is low attaining?** The reality is that children can fall behind in their learning for all sorts of reasons. Perhaps they have not been attending school? Perhaps they have recently moved to the country and have not yet learnt to understand English? Perhaps they are experiencing change or trauma which is impacting on their ability to access learning opportunities? Perhaps the learning opportunities are not effectively differentiated, or the quality of teaching is less than effective? Or perhaps the child has a 'learning difficulty or disability that calls for special educational provision', which is the definition of SEN used in the Code of Practice 2015. In other words, **having a special educational need is only one reason why a child may fall behind with learning, so not every child who is falling behind necessarily has SEN**.

There is also a need to identify learners who are disabled and those with a medical need. It is important to recognise that although the abbreviations SEN and D are often combined, this can refer to *three* groups of children. SEN refers to those with a 'learning difficulty or disability that calls for special educational provision', and D refers to those pupils who are disabled as defined in the Equality Act 2010. SEND are those pupils who have both a learning difficulty and are disabled according to the Equality Act 2010 definition which says that a person is disabled if they have

> **a physical or mental impairment which has a long-term and substantial adverse effect on their ability to carry out normal day-to-day activities.**

It is important to note that, within this definition, 'long-term' is defined as one year and one day and 'substantial' in the law is defined as 'not trivial.' The implication of this is significant. For example, if a child broke both of their legs and was required to use a wheelchair for six to ten weeks, they would not 'legally' be defined as disabled. As such the 'legal' duties outlined in the Equality Act 2010 would not be necessary for a school or setting to follow unless the child were to become disabled a year and one day later. (That said I have not met the school or staff member who would not make reasonable adjustments in such a context!) There would however be duties placed on the school or setting to meet the child's medical needs, under the Children and Families Act 2014. This Act states that all schools and settings are required to make arrangements to support any medical need. This is why it is essential that SENCOs and SEN Practitioners use the SEND Code of Practice to inform practice regarding SEND, the Equality Act 2010 to inform practice regarding Disabled learners (and other protected characteristics) and the current DfE guidance on medical needs. If you or your staff are not completely confident and clear about the requirements in these documents, it is essential that this is immediately addressed as part of your Continued Professional Development (CPD) programme. The Centre for Studies in Inclusive Education (CSIE) have developed an excellent resource which provides an overview of the responsibilities of schools and settings as outlined by the Equality Act.

To summarise, a child can be disabled and have SEN (SEN-D), but a child can be disabled and *not* have a learning difficulty that requires special provision (D.) Equally they can be a child who has a learning difficulty that requires special provision but do *not* have a physical or mental impairment which has a long-term substantial adverse effect on their ability to carry out normal day to day activities (SEN). A child could also have a medical condition, but not have SEN or be disabled, (MN) or indeed have a medical condition and SEN and be disabled, (SEN-D/MN). This is summarised in the SEN Profile Venn Diagram.

A blank proforma of this diagram is included in this chapter, as this could be a useful way to capture the numbers and/or percentages of learners in each category. It is also a useful visual reminder of the need to be clear and consistent about how and why these categories are applied to children and young people.

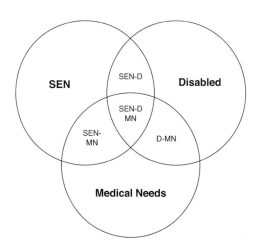

Prior to undertaking any additional assessment activity, it is essential for the SENCO or SEN Practitioner to have clarity and confidence with their system of identifying those learners with SEN, SEND, D and/or medical needs. The SEN record, whatever form it takes, is useful for capturing identified learners, but accurate identification is vital. SENCOs and SEN Practitioners may attend 'progress meetings' alongside other staff in order to discuss emerging concerns regarding those learners who are not making expected curriculum progress. This may or may not be because they have SEN and delayed curriculum progress should not be the only factor in identifying a child as having SEN. Equally, expected curriculum progress does not mean that a learner does not have SEN. For example, a learner with autism may be high functioning and achieve great curriculum success but be experiencing huge social anxiety or isolation during play and lunchtimes. This could be indicative of a 'special' educational need.

To promote greater clarity regarding identification of needs, an SEN profile sheet has been developed. Please note that this is an SEN and not a SEND profile sheet, as it does not include information about those learners who are disabled according to the Equality Act 2010. Similarly, it does not include those with medical needs, or indeed others from disadvantaged or vulnerable groups. This information is expanded in the SEN record, Disabled record and Medical Needs record, which are also included with completed examples from the fictitious 'Willow school'.

Implications for SENCOs and SEN Practitioners

The ultimate implication for SENCOs and SEN Practitioners is to ensure clarity of identification of need. Do not let 'SEN' or 'SEND' become shorthand for any learner who is falling behind in learning. Of course, it is essential that we address the needs presented by all learners, but do not let yourself or other staff simply assume that the learner has SEN or SEND. They might, but there might be another explanation such as English being a second language, or they have a history of persistent absence. They might also be low attaining and therefore need opportunities to boost their learning, but they are making progress. If they have a 'learning difficulty that requires special educational provision' then yes, absolutely identify them as having SEN. **Remember however, for every child or young person you identify as having SEN, you are saying that they require special provision that is 'additional or different' from the differentiated curriculum. Therefore, you must be able to account for this for all learners identified with SEN.** You must also be able to demonstrate how you 'assess, plan, do and review' this SEN Support.

SEND Profile

The purpose of gathering the SEND profile information is to capture an overview of the numbers and percentages of children and young people identified with SEN, those who are Disabled and those with a medical need. A learner can have SEN, or be Disabled, or have a Medical Need. Equally they could have a combination of these, as presented in the diagram below. Clarification regarding the numbers of learners within each category is essential to plan appropriate SEN provision, to make reasonable adjustments and to provide necessary aids or support. This overview will also help to ensure that resources and training are directed to the most appropriate areas of need.

Defining SEN, D and MN

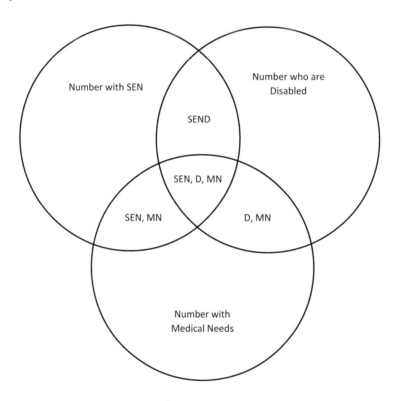

Identification of your SEN Profile

Record the numbers of learners receiving SEN Support and those with an EHCP. Calculate the percentage against the school population. Select ONE of the four categories of need, (Cognition & Learning, Communication & Interaction, Social, Emotional & Mental Health or Physical and Sensory), using a 'best fit' approach, to describe the provision that is offered. Individual learning needs may of course cross more than one category, but for this purpose, select one. Calculate the numbers and percentages for each category.

SEND Profile

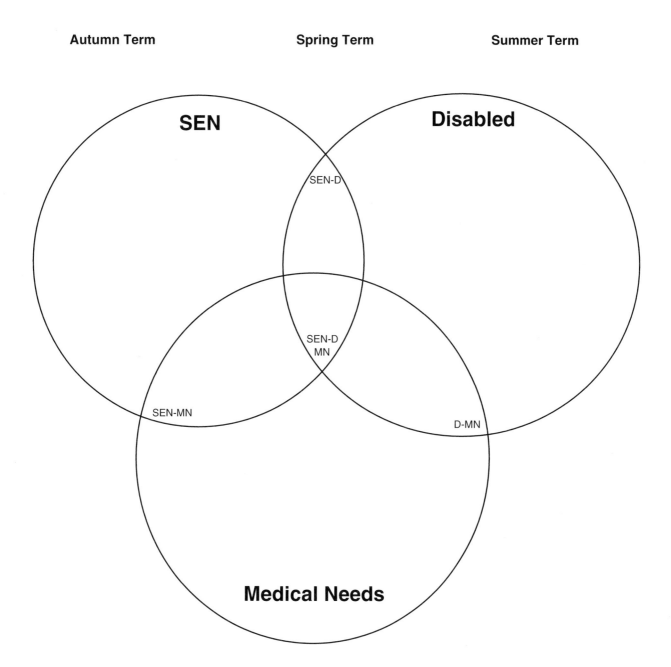

Autumn Term   **Spring Term**   **Summer Term**

Key definitions

A child has a special educational need if they have a learning difficulty that requires special educational provision. (Code of Practice 2014)

A person is disabled if they have 'a physical or mental impairment which has a long-term and substantial adverse effect on their ability to carry out normal day-to-day activities'. (Equality Act 2010)

Our Primary School SEN Profile

Term:

	Our School Number	Our School Percentage	National Percentage
Total pupils with SEN			
Total pupils with EHCP			
Total pupils at SEN Support			
	SEN Support	EHCP	Year Group Total
Year R			
Year 1			
Year 2			
Year 3			
Year 4			
Year 5			
Year 6			

Year Group Distribution of Pupils at SEN Support

	Cognition and Learning	Communication and Interaction	Social, Emotional and Mental Health	Physical and/ or Sensory
Year R				
Year 1				
Year 2				
Year 3				
Year 4				
Year 5				
Year 6				

Our Secondary School SEN Profile

Term:

	Our School Number	Our School Percentage	National Percentage
Total pupils with SEN			
Total pupils with EHCP			
Total pupils at SEN Support			
	SEN Support	EHCP	Year Group Total
Year 7			
Year 8			
Year 9			
Year 10			
Year 11			
Year 12			
Year 13			

Year Group Distribution of Pupils at SEN Support

	Cognition and Learning	Communication and Interaction	Social, Emotional and Mental Health	Physical and/or Sensory
Year 7				
Year 8				
Year 9				
Year 10				
Year 11				
Year 12				
Year 13				

Willow School SEN Record Example

Name	Date of Birth	Year Group	Census Category	Code of Practice	Category of Need	Barriers to Learning	Provision Map/ ILP/ IBP/One Page Profile	Parent/ Carer Informed	Review Cycle or Annual Review Date	Additional Needs (Disabled, PP, Medical Needs, LAC, EAL)
Harry Baker	8–12–10	2	MLD	SEN Support	C&L	Working Memory Writing Reading	PM	Yes	Termly	N/A
Joanne Clarke	6–11–10	2	HI	EHCP	P/S, C&I	Mobility Independence HI Communication	ILP, OPP	Yes	AR: 6-6-18	Disabled
Chloe Jones	23–7–08	4	SLCN	SEN Support	C&I	Speech Language	ILP, PM	Yes	Termly	LAC
Khalid Khan	14-4-07	5	BESD	SEN Support	SEMH	Self-esteem Anger	IBP	Yes	Fortnightly	N/A

Our School SEN Record

Name	Date of Birth	Year Group	Census Category	Code of Practice	Category of Need	Barriers to Learning	Provision Map/ ILP/ One-Page Profile	Parent/ Carer Informed	Review Date	Additional Needs (Disabled, PP, Medical Needs)

Willow School Disabled Pupil Record – Example

Name	Date of Birth	Year Group	Impairment	Reasonable Adjustments	Parent/ Carer Liaison	Support Services (Physio, OT, CAMHS)	Additional Needs (SEN, PP, LAC, EAL)
Sangeeta Majid	3-5-14	3	Cerebral Palsy – limited mobility and speech	Personal Assistant supports mobility and personal care, use of communication aid	Half-termly meetings	Physio, SALT, OT	EHCP- C&I, C&L, P/S
Kyle Davis	12-4-11	6	ADHD – daily medication	Frequent exercise breaks, shorter tasks, lunchtime play leader scheme	Half-termly meetings	ADHD nurse	None
Annie Jones	8-11-15	2	Mobility issues – wheelchair user	Ensure access to site and ground floor classroom.	As requested by parent	Physio	None
Samuel Leopold	3-9-17	R	Hearing impairment	Makaton sign, visual bell, visual toys	Half-termly	Sensory Support Service	SEN Support

Our School Disabled Pupil Record

Name	Date of Birth	Year Group	Impairment	Reasonable Adjustments	Parent/ Carer Liaison	Support Services (Physio, OT, CAMHS)	Additional Needs (SEN, PP, LAC, EAL Disabled)

Willow School Pupils with Medical Needs – Example

Name	Date of Birth	Year Group	Medical Need	Medication	Care Plan	Parent/ Carer Liaison	Additional Needs (SEN, PP, LAC, EAL Disabled)								
Lucy Davidson	11-3-11	5	Diabetes	Insulin 3 times a day	1-9-17 in medical room	Half-termly	None								
David Edwards	22-4-16	2	Asthma	Inhaler as required	12-4-16 in medical room	As required	None								
Nathan Clarke	3-10-19	1	Epilepsy	Taken at home	24-1-16 in medical room	Half-termly	SEN Support								

Our School Pupils with Medical Needs

Name	Date of Birth	Year Group	Medical Need	Medication	Care Plan	Parent/Carer Liaison	Additional Needs (SEN, PP, LAC, EAL Disabled)

Reflections...

- How confident are you and colleagues in identifying learners with SEN, SEND, D and or MN?
- Can you distinguish between SEN Support (that is additional to or different from the differentiated curriculum) and curriculum attainment 'booster' or 'catch-up' groups?
- Are all staff and governors aware of your SEN profile? Is this outlined in your SEN information report?

References

Equality: Making it Happen – A Guide to Help Schools Ensure Everyone is Safe, Included and Learning (2016) Centre for Studies in Inclusive Education.

Special Educational Needs and Disability Code of Practice: 0 to 25 Years – Statutory Guidance for Organisations which Work with and Support Children and Young People who have Special Educational Needs or Disabilities (2014; updated 2015) Department for Education and Department of Health.

4. Developing a shared language of assessment

Often in education our shared language of assessment is of course our curriculum. It contains our collaborative intent for teaching and learning across a breadth of subjects. Schools and settings work hard to develop a clear and purposeful curriculum and are able to articulate the rationale for its design or intent, implementation and impact. Curriculum entitlement is the right of all learners and it is essential that as SENCOs and SEN Practitioners, we continue to ensure that this entitlement remains accessible to all. **SEN assessment is not seeking to provide an alternative or replacement to the curriculum, but rather to inform 'additional or different' requirements that will ultimately support learning and *increase access* to the curriculum.** However, to identify the 'additional or different' requirements we need to have a language of assessment that goes *beyond* the curriculum. Of course, curriculum assessment is the right of all learners and the responsibility of all educators, but when a learner is identified as having SEN, then 'additional or different' information is required alongside the curriculum. **Yet often, we continue to assess only against the curriculum.**

If a learner is experiencing difficulties with maths, this will of course be identified by their teacher. It could be raised at a progress meeting and 'collaborative learning' of maths could be offered. Where the difficulty has arisen because the learner has 'missed' some aspects of maths, then this is likely to be highly effective. (The Education Endowment Foundation Teaching and Learning Toolkit rate collaborative learning as +5 and describe it as providing 'moderate impact for very low cost based on extensive evidence'.) However, if the difficulty arises because the learner has a particular barrier to learning, *'more of the same'*, whether it is collaborative or not, may not be effective. The role of the SENCO and SEN Practitioner in many ways is to support teachers to consider the reasons *why* a learner may be experiencing difficulties with, in this case, maths. What are the barriers that are limiting learning? With regards to maths, it could be that the key difficulty for the learner links to language. They may not understand the question or indeed the instruction. Similarly, the learner may have a small working memory, so they are struggling to 'hold' and manipulate information. They may also have a slow speed of processing, so they need more time to assimilate information and genuinely struggle to keep up with the pace of information during the lesson. Or they may have short attention and are therefore unable to sustain focus in order to access information. (These barriers may also limit the impact of 'collaborative learning', as this approach requires effective use of language, memory, processing and attention.)

There are so many possible explanations or hypotheses about the barriers to learning that are at that time the learner's 'special' educational need. It is the identification of these barriers that should form the content of SEN assessment, remembering, of course, that curriculum assessment is going on anyway *and should continue*, but SEN assessment is 'additional to' this. It may be useful for some staff to consider curriculum assessment as the 'day job' and additional, targeted SEN assessment as 'overtime'. An employee cannot just do overtime without having fulfilled the day job first! **The promotion of SEN assessment here is not an alternative to curriculum assessment; it is based on the assumption that curriculum assessment is already going on effectively and will continue.** The additional SEN assessment is intended to reveal greater information, or to help identify a working hypothesis about the barriers that appear to be negatively impacting on learning for that child or young person at that time.

For many colleagues, it is the apparent absence of a shared language of barriers to learning that can lead to SEN assessment simply becoming 'more' curriculum assessment. Staff do not always have access to a systematic approach for SEN assessment. If a learner is experiencing difficulties with reading, a reading assessment will take place. If they are finding writing difficult, an assessment of writing will take place. This is useful but will not, in itself, necessarily help to reveal the speech and language barrier that may be limiting the learner's access to writing, or the phonological awareness difficulty that is limiting access to reading. Developing a consistent and shared language of barriers to learning is an essential element for planning SEN assessment.

There is not a single or 'definitive' list of barriers to learning. Instead, it is our role to attempt to hypothesise what these are, informed by additional assessment (not just curricular performance,) and in partnership with parents/carers and the learner themselves. There are some excellent tools and resources that can be used to evaluate skills such as speech, language, working memory, speed of processing, listening, comprehension, phonological awareness as well as motivation, attention, fear of failure and resiliency. Many of these are standardised, but SENCOs and SEN Practitioners can develop their own. After all, the purpose of the assessment is to establish a baseline or starting point which will inform future action.

The purpose of 'future action' is to either overcome or where possible to remove barriers to learning. It is important to acknowledge that for some learners, they experience barriers which cannot be removed. This is particularly true for some disabled learners or those with medical needs. In that case, the focus is upon overcoming or reducing the impact of the barrier to enable access to learning. However, for some learners, the ultimate goal will be to remove the barrier itself. For example, if a learner is not yet able to read independently, reading is their current barrier to learning. During a science lesson, action will be taken to overcome this barrier. It could be that the learner works with a peer who is able to read the instructions to them, or an adult reads information to them, thus temporarily overcoming that barrier, enabling their access to the science learning opportunity. At some point however, action will be taken to try to teach the learner to read, thus ultimately removing the barrier to learning. This is more likely to take place as an intervention or a targeted action outside of the science lesson.

Clarity regarding identified barriers to learning is the purpose of SEN assessment. Once the barrier is identified, consideration can be given to action that could overcome and/or remove the barrier for that learner. All actions informed by assessment should include a description of the *anticipated impact* of the action, and then, over time, the *actual impact* of the action. The actual impact then itself becomes part of the assessment information used to inform the next action that is required, hence our focus on the 'assess, plan, do and review' cycle.

Implications for SENCOs and SEN Practitioners

The first implication is to consider whether you and staff have a shared understanding of the language of barriers to learning, or in fact, do you/they tend to describe need using diagnostic labels? Diagnostic labels tend to be medical in nature and as such are predominantly made by health professionals. We must guard against the tendency to use medical labels or diagnoses before any such diagnosis has been made. Furthermore, we must ensure that our colleagues do not tell a parent or carer that they think the child might have autism or dyspraxia. **These are medical diagnoses and as educationalists, we do not diagnose. Of course, we identify concerns and we talk to our children and families about barriers we see. We ask if similar observations have been seen at home, but we must describe the barriers rather than applying a diagnosis.** For example, instead of declaring that a child may have autism, talk about the observed barriers to learning linked to social communication and or social interaction. Talk about the evidence of anxiety and rigid views. And, if and when necessary, discuss the potential involvement of a health professional to consider if there is a medical explanation for these difficulties. This is far more relevant for families than the casual and potentially inaccurate referencing of diagnostic labels.

Diagnostic labels also tend to convey minimal information for teachers, unless the teacher has extensive knowledge of that particular diagnosis. For example, informing a teacher that a learner has dyspraxia does not help the teacher to plan (unless they have knowledge of dyspraxia.) In contrast, informing a teacher that a learner experiences difficulties with sequencing, fine motor co-ordination including writing, working memory and organisation, immediately flags the areas that the learner may struggle with. **The next step and indeed key implication for SENCOs and SEN Practitioners is to audit the knowledge and confidence of staff regarding the changes or adjustments they should make having received this information.** Do your teachers have knowledge and access to alternative means of recording for learners? Do they know how to support a learner with a small working memory? And do you know if this actually happens in the classroom?

Creating a shared language of barriers to learning enables communication regarding action that can be taken to overcome and/or remove these barriers. The grids that follow are presented as starting points to encourage your thinking about these two concepts and to promote reflection on the action you take. For example, how much SEN time and resources are spent on action that seeks to *overcome* barriers compared to action that seeks to *remove* barriers? How does this action impact on learner independence? Do you define the 'anticipated' and 'actual' impact of an action? Could you?

Overcoming and Removing Barriers to Learning: Cognition & Learning

Barrier to Learning	Strategies to Overcome	Strategies to Remove
Remembering instructions (Working Memory)	Mind mapping, paraphrase work instructions, key word prompts, voice recording of instructions	Targeted memory games and activities e.g.: digit span and object recall
Reading & Spelling	Provide key word list, use electronic presentation of words, e.g. clicker, adult or child reader, audio books	Daily rehearsal of sounds targeting fluency and accuracy, individual reading and spelling programme
Handwriting	Writing slope, pencil grips, voice recorder, vlogging, photos, typing	Fine motor skills, isolated circular, vertical and horizontal mark making, touch typing,
Speed of Processing	Additional time, advanced warning of questioning	Reaction time activities, fluency games against the clock
Number Sequencing	Use of number line, Numicon & other visual aids	Daily rehearsal of sequencing number cubes, puzzles, beads
Planning & Organising	Adult or peer supporter, structured questions, now and next, lists and reminder alarms	Mind mapping, topic webs, now and next, story boards
Fear of Failure	Encouragement, rewards, reassurance	Experience of success, '5 lives' approach, CBT techniques linked to 'being wrong'

Overcoming and Removing Barriers to Learning: Communication & Interaction

Barrier to Learning	Strategies to Overcome	Strategies to Remove
Speech (expressive vocabulary)	Use of picture cards or word banks, objects of reference, Makaton. Key phrase cards	Targeted intervention from SALT and use of Key vocabulary cards, sentence starters, talking partners
Language (receptive vocabulary)	Visually demonstrate work expectations, work with positive peer model, use of objects	Individual programme planned by SALT to include category words, subject words
Answering Questions	Visual prompts or paddles to indicate view, preparation time, closed questions	Explicit teaching and rehearsal of responding to questions – identification of key words
Social Communication	Adult mediator, peer support, visual prompts, key phrases, e.g. "Can I play?"	Social stories, explicit teaching and rehearsal of verbal & non-verbal communication skills
Social Interaction	Adult mediator to 'broker' responses from others. Sign-posting and appeasing	Use social stories and scenarios to rehearse possible responses
Making Friends	Friendship stop, circle of friends, adult mediator, targeted interest groups	Teach and rehearse social skills, social stories
Keeping Up with 'Banter'	Peer buddy, established friendships, shared play activities	Language games, rehearsal of questions and answers

Overcoming and Removing Barriers to Learning: Social, Emotional & Mental Health

Barrier to Learning	Strategies to Overcome	Strategies to Remove
Low Self-esteem	Noticing success, positive feedback, praise	Self-identification of successes
Low Confidence/ Fear of Failure	'5 lives', whiteboard, have a go book	Positive experience of success and management of 'failure'
High Anxiety	Peer support, rehearsal, advanced warning, visual timetables	Cognitive behavioural techniques exploring anxious associations
Low Resilience	Praise, intervention prior to failure, peer support	Targeted activities such as *Bouncing Back and Coping with Change*, by Tina Rae, 2016
Obsessional	Visual timetable, advanced warning of change	CBT techniques exploring anxious associations
Limited Self-regulation	Adult mentor, direct incident intervention, time out or exit cards	Language of emotions, teaching of 'signals', social stories, rehearsal and role play
Anger	Adult mentor, direct incident intervention, time out or exit cards	Teaching of 'signals', explicit teaching of strategies to apply, mindfulness techniques, mood diaries

Overcoming and Removing Barriers to Learning: Physical & Sensory

Barrier to Learning	Strategies to Overcome	Strategies to Remove
Organisation	Now and next visual structure, pictorial boards	Explicit teaching of Mind-mapping, lists, timetabling
Sequencing	Post-its to prompt and sequence, use of visual structures	Explicit teaching of sequential rules, rehearsals of tasks
Visual Impairment	Audio books, peer supporter, audio description	Teaching of Braille, appropriately personalised print, voice software
Hearing Impairment	Visual prompts, peer supporter	British Sign Language, hearing aid, cochlear implant
Fine & Gross Motor Skills	Adult or peer mediator to support tasks, audio recording, typing, pencil grips, adaptive equipment	Activities to increase distal muscle control, e.g., pincer tasks, colouring, cutting, threading. Physio or occupational therapy programme to develop fluency with movements
Mobility	Avoid 'busy' times leaving sessions early, adult or peer supporter	Independent use of mobility aids, physio programme where identified by Health
Sensory Processing	Strategies to screen out sensory information, e.g.: headphones, glasses, working at work station.	Individually targeted programme of sensory experiences to aid integration

Anticipated and Actual Impact Aspirations for my Learners at SEN Support – Autumn term

Pupil Name	What I would like to be different for them…	What is actually different…	Priority Next Steps

Aspirations for my Learners at SEN Support – Spring term

Pupil Name	What I would like to be different for them...	What is actually different...	Priority Next Steps

Aspirations for my Learners at SEN Support – Summer term

Pupil Name	What I would like to be different for them…	What is actually different…	Priority Next Steps

Reflections...

- Do you and colleagues have a shared language of assessment regarding barriers to learning?
- How do you assess needs that require provision that is 'additional or different' from a differentiated curriculum?
- Does the SEN Support offered in the school primarily seek to overcome or remove barriers to learning?

Reference

The Education Endowment Foundation Teaching and Learning Toolkit (2020) Available at https://educationendowmentfoundation.org.uk/ (Accessed 13 September 2020)

5. The 7 Cs Learning Portfolio

The 7 Cs Learning Portfolio was developed from direct work with children, young people, families and staff. As an Educational Psychologist I engage in many conversations about learning, the majority of which tend to begin with descriptions of curriculum strengths and difficulties. Concerns are frequently expressed in terms of subjects and the action taken by schools also described in relation to additional curriculum tasks. Often my focus would be upon identifying the learning profile of the child or young person, working directly with them and in consultation with staff and their parents or carers. This helps to generate a working hypothesis of strengths and barriers to learning which, in turn, identifies next steps and action that is 'additional to or different from the differentiated curriculum'.

It became clear however that **as educators we lacked a 'shared' language of assessment and often our tests and tasks were not flexible enough to capture the strengths and interests of a child.** I am reminded of a wonderful 7-year-old, who experienced a range of barriers to learning, identified by the combined standardised tests and dynamic assessment tasks we shared, but who, more importantly, 'transformed' when I asked him what he thought he was good at. This young learner 'lit up' and became animated and confident as he described himself as a "junk modeller!" It was a privilege to listen to him describe in detail his recent construction and the plans he had for his next model. I was struck by the contrast in his discussion about this topic compared to his lessons and was mindful that despite the extensive array of assessment tools available to me, I was not able to 'capture' this brilliant skill within any of them. At the same time, many SENCOs expressed frustration and uncertainty about what interventions could be offered that are 'additional to or different' from a differentiated curriculum, as required by the SEND Code of Practice (2014; updated 2015), for learners at SEN Support. **It was clear that if assessment was only made against the curriculum, intervention could only be informed by the curriculum.** As such, how was this 'additional to or different from the differentiated curriculum' and not simply more of the same?

The 7 Cs Learning Portfolio provides a framework for holistic assessment of skills and attributes that contribute to accessing the curriculum. It is also diverse enough to promote the identification of strengths in all learners. **It has been written primarily to support learners who may be identified as having a special educational need and receiving SEN Support.** It also provides a framework for intervention or targeted action that is 'additional to or different from' the differentiated curriculum. This means progress can be explicitly anticipated and the actual progress can be measured. A Progress Tracker to support the demonstration of impact has also been written to complement this process.

The 7 Cs Learning Portfolio is a *language* of assessment. It provides a framework that encourages dialogue between the teacher, learner and parent/carer, intended to inform an evaluation of the child or young person as a 'whole' learner. It can be applied in one of three ways. The first is the 'functional' or light touch approach. This is where the SENCO or teacher uses the language of the 7 Cs within their existing work and framework. It can simply be integrated as a prompt to aid discussion. The second or 'intermediate' level is the medium touch approach. Here the language is used alongside the prepared action sheets or learner leaflets which would replace existing SEN Support records. The third or 'extensive' level is the 'heavy' touch approach, as the entire 7 Cs Learning Portfolio would be introduced to a learner and used throughout the academic year. The Pupil Portfolio would become an annual 'self- assessment' tool or record and each of the 7 Cs would be explored with the learner either in their entirety or 'chunked' as deemed relevant.

As the name suggests, the 7 Cs Learning Portfolio consists of seven areas of learning, each beginning with the letter C. Within each area there are seven elements, so a total of 49 themes for consideration. This does *not* mean that you assess against all 49 themes at once, but rather you refer to the 49 themes as a framework for reviewing the learning profile of a child or young person. (In the same way as you would not attempt to use *all* of the words that you know when engaging in a conversation, you would not use all of the 49 themes during one review, but you do have access to them!) Similarly, you do not have to use all of the language in this framework for every child, but it is there to aid and prompt you.

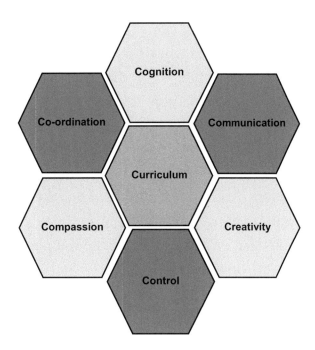

Within the 7 Cs framework, the curriculum is at the centre of the model as it is the entitlement of all children and young people. The additional six themes: **Cognition, Communication, Creativity, Control, Compassion** and **Co-ordination** are considered essential in order to maximise access to the curriculum. The descriptors below are intended to prompt and guide the adult facilitating the learning conversation or SEN Support meeting to consider the array of potential strengths and areas for development. Ultimately, with the learner and their parent/carers, the teacher should identify three strengths and three areas for development (or current barriers to learning) that will inform future action.

Cognition

Within the theme of Cognition (meaning thinking), consideration is given to the pupil's strengths and barriers to learning that relate to specific areas of cognition. These include:

1 **Working Memory** – Working memory is different to other types of memory and can be considered as the capacity to 'hold' and manipulate information. It is almost the information before it goes into storage. Auditory working memory as measured using a digit-span recall-type task, can indicate capacity to hold 'verbal' information such as when listening to instructions. Visual working memory as measured using recall of pictures or images, can be used when copying information from the board. It can be useful to consider working memory as 'capacity' rather than as 'good or bad'. For example, consider a spectrum of containers which have

increasing capacity to hold water. An egg cup, glass, jug, vase, bucket and barrel each have differing amounts of water that they can hold. This is similar to an individual's working memory capacity. Some people may have a small glass-size capacity, others may have a bucket-sized capacity. Gathercole and Alloway, in their excellent book called *Working Memory in the Classroom* argue that up until the age of 14 a child may improve their capacity to hold information slightly, perhaps increasing from an egg cup to a glass for example. But it would be unlikely that they would move from an egg cup to a barrel. And once a child exceeds the age of 14 years old, they tend to keep the capacity they have. As such, our focus needs to be on efficiency of working memory, aids that will support and an awareness of how realistic the demands of tasks are on working memory.

2. **Speed of Processing** – This refers to the time taken to assimilate or take on board information. Our capacity to assimilate and interpret information and the time taken to do this, can be highly significant to our ability to follow and absorb information during a lesson or when reading individually. In reality, if we have a slower speed of processing, we may perceive that the pace of information is moving too quickly and, we may struggle to keep up. Needing more time to assimilate information can also impact on friendships as learners may struggle to keep up with conversation or peer 'banter'. Similarly, if speed of processing is a strength and a learner has a fast speed of processing, they may move on more quickly and become frustrated and potentially distracted.

3. **Inference** – This cognitive skill relates to our ability to use information and to extract meaning in order to make predictions. This is an executive or higher order functioning skill, and one that is essential to aid insight and application of learning. Learners are asked to infer meaning from text, conversation or direct engagement, but to do this they must 'notice' the information, extracting key aspects and then apply these aspects to possible implications.

4. **Anticipation** – Anticipation is the skill of pausing, considering and identifying possible outcomes and responding accordingly. Often this requires a delay in response in order to consider and evaluate options or implications. Learners are required to regulate any impulsive responses and to visualise or hypothesise consequences or implications. It can involve the application of prior experiences as well as an evaluation of the likelihood of a particular outcome.

5. **Reflection** – Reflective practice by adults or children involves noticing and considering actions and their impact. Conscious 'noticing' or 'recalling' involves

sequencing and organisation as well as 'labelling' and language. Learners who reflect are asked to 'look back' and to consider actions with the benefit of hindsight. They may wish to identify lessons they consider they have learnt and whether they would act in the same way again.

6. **Evaluation** – The skill of evaluation utilises the skill of reflection and requires the process of weighing up and making judgements. Such critique requires a perception of criteria and intended objectives. It also requires a confidence in one's own worth and capacity to offer an evaluation, as well as the ability to express this.

7. **Analysis** – Analysis is the skill of isolating and or combining information against different criteria to extract further information. If children and young people are able to apply the skills of analysis, they are able to form a view which may help them to express their developing perspective. They are able to identify similarities and differences and extract information from these.

Communication

The theme of Communication requires consideration to the pupil's strengths and barriers in relation to:

1. **Expressive Vocabulary** – Expressive vocabulary is the 'pool' or number of words known and used by a learner. These words enable the expression of ideas, emotions and speech. A learner may attempt to describe objects rather than naming them and they may need additional time to find specific words. For example, a child may say "you know, it has red and black spots" and an adult or peer may say "a ladybird?" And the learner says, "yes a ladybird". When evaluating this area, it may be useful to consider the following questions:
   • Can the learner talk fluently and variedly using subject and category words?
   • Do they have an age-appropriate vocabulary and are they able to identify, name and describe objects accordingly?
   • Can they name words and objects and answer questions?

2. **Articulation** – This skill relates specifically to the accuracy of pronunciation and the clarity of spoken sounds. It may be that the learner finds it hard to say a particular word or sound. This could impact on their ability to be understood as well as their ability to recall and hear sounds in words, as they may retrieve a

'different' sound when they say it. A child may also have a stutter or may stumble when pronouncing specific sounds.

3. **Language and Comprehension** – When considering this aspect of learning, consideration is given to the child or young person's capacity to understand spoken or written language. It is interesting to note that some children who find language difficult to understand will attempt to dominate conversations and will talk incessantly about topics of interest. Intentionally or unintentionally, this can result in adults seeking to 'move away' from the chattering child or adult failure in getting a word in edgeways! An effective strategy to promote the avoidance of language that may not be understood. It is also important to note that a learner may be able to identify individual words in isolation but they may struggle to extract the meaning of key words when presented in sentences (known as oral discourse comprehension).

4. **Collaborative Conversation** – This theme is included as a way of recognising that conversation involves more than the simple application of spoken words. It requires turn-taking in speech as well as the capacity to respond or ask questions, adapting one's own contribution in light of what has just been heard. It also requires social understanding of communication and the value of a collaborative exchange.

5. **Listening** – Listening is not the same skill as hearing. Listening involves attending and extracting information from speech to ascertain a view or perspective expressed. It requires focus and attention as well as the identification of the meaning of key words. It also requires motivation and a desire to listen as part of a social interaction.

6. **Social Communication (Output)** – Social communication and social interaction are often used interchangeably specifically when referring to children with autism. However, it can be useful to consider the two skills as different. Social communication is defined here as the use of verbal and or non-verbal communication for expression, i.e., the skills used to 'output' communication. This includes an awareness of one's own personal space, the use of eye contact and initiating conversation.

7. **Social Interaction (Input)** – Social interaction is defined here as the reaction and or response to verbal and non-verbal communication from others, i.e. communication that is received as 'input'. This includes reacting to comments from others, jokes, humour, personal space as well as responding to a question or comment within a social exchange.

Creativity

In this theme consideration is given to the pupil's strengths and barriers relating to:

1. **Generation of Ideas –**What a wonderful skill it is, to be able to generate and share original ideas and thoughts. From my experience many children and young people have original and at times 'random' or quirky thoughts, revealing a capacity to think outside of the box. Yet do we currently assess or value this? Or are we more likely to redirect them to the 'fact' we are attempting to teach them? This theme encourages the active 'noticing' of ideas and suggestions and the 'connections' that the learner has made across topics.

2. **Problem-solving –**This skill requires using initiative to find and sometimes create solutions. One of the greatest privileges associated with working with children is the opportunity to hear how they would 'resolve' problems including perhaps avoiding the creation of the 'problem' in the first place. This skill involves the application and adaptation of prior knowledge to achieve a specific outcome.

3. **Attention –** Attention involves sustained focus and the ability to exclude or filter other sources of noise or information. Often we focus on attention as a missing or underdeveloped attribute, yet rarely we define or value it as a skill for learning, instead taking it for granted or assuming it as a 'given'. Those who have the capacity to sustain focus and concentration are able to maximise learning opportunities independently or with others. It is an incredible skill but one that is predominantly referenced when in 'deficit'. Its inclusion within the 7 Cs is intended to encourage recognition of it as a strength as well as for those where it is an area for development.

4. **Motivation –** This refers to an eagerness and willingness to engage. Motivation can of course be extrinsic or intrinsic, implying that the trigger for participation is either linked to factors within the child or young person or are external or tangible factors such as the view of others or a specific consequence or reward. Sustaining motivation when a task is challenging or not deemed of huge relevance or interest is a significant skill.

5. **Making Things –** This skill refers to a tangible 'gift', skill or interest associated with construction or crafting. Junk modelling, sewing, baking, cooking, woodwork, Lego models, crafting and self-directed construction, art or design are all examples of the application of this skill. Indeed, many young fans of 'Minecraft' attribute their motivation to the creativity of building things within this IT

platform. Children, young people and adults, will often design and construct their own creations or perhaps follow instructions, a template or a pattern to replicate something using a range of materials or stimuli.

6. **Courage and Determination –** This theme acknowledges the attribute of courage and determination, defined here as being 'fearless to have a go' and sustain effort. As educators we often forget that learning involves risk, and for children and young people we ask them to engage with us and enter into the new and unknown every day! So many will join us in this 'adventure' that we may forget that this is a significant request requiring courage and determination, trust and resilience.

7. **Trust –** Trust is at the heart of education both for adults and children, yet it has become an unspoken assumption. Our children who do not trust enough to 'risk' learning with us and who exhibit a fear of failure or a defiant refusal to participate, explicitly remind us why trust is an essential attribute that we should identify, assess and value. Trust requires security and the perception of safety and value. It is key to the formation and sustainment of relationships.

Control

The theme of control requires consideration to the pupil's strengths and barriers in relation to:

1. **Self-regulation –** This skill refers to the ability to control and manage behaviour, language, thoughts and emotions. We often prioritise the ability to regulate behaviour as this is visible and can be associated with risk and safety. However, alongside this are the skills of managing language, thoughts and emotions. The reality with self-regulation is that when it is implemented effectively, we tend to not 'notice' it. For children and young people who lack self-regulation, we will prioritise it for development, but once it is achieved, we may not ever comment on it, despite the fact that it is a lifelong skill that requires daily rehearsal and application. Including this within the 7 Cs Model is intended to remind us to 'credit' children and young people who have this as a strength, as well as to target the development of the skill where necessary.

2. **Behaviour for Learning –** This attribute can be defined as a readiness to engage and participate in learning tasks. Readiness is an interesting word as it implies an ability to react or respond on demand. For children and young people, it demands an ability to switch between thoughts or tasks and follow direction. It assumes

many of the skills already explored such as listening, attention, motivation and language, as well as an understanding of the collaborative exchange that takes place between the teacher or TA and the child themselves. Once again it is often only defined when it is in deficit and is taken for granted when it is present. If we are to review learners at a holistic level, it is essential that this is part of our criteria.

3. **Anxiety Management** – The skill of managing anxiety is an attribute of an effective learner, as they are able to retain control over fear and manage their experience of anxious thoughts. For many, the curriculum and learning represent the potential for failure as they are new and diverse by definition. To retain control over anxiety and to manage a 'fear of failure' and continue to pursue the unknown is a wonderful attribute worthy of our consideration and recognition.

4. **Confidence** – To function with confidence is to function. A strong belief in oneself and one's own capacity to contribute is an incredible asset for learning and indeed life. Those learners with confidence are able to attempt tasks and are able to grow both from success and failure as they experience these with the full knowledge of their existing skills. Confidence develops with a positive sense of self, value and worth (esteem.) It also requires management to avoid 'inflation' and misplacement, which can be detrimental to the learner and those around them.

5. **Resilience** – This refers to the capacity to 'bounce back' and try again. Resilience can be considered as a renewable energy source which becomes depleted but can be replenished. For some, however, the rate of depletion exceeds that of replenishment and as such they lose the capacity to bounce back. This is not a failing of the individual but a failing of their access to sources of replenishment. We must credit those who present with resiliency and support those who do not by facilitating their replenishment.

6. **Language of Emotions** – Fluency and accuracy with a language of emotions enables expression and understanding of feelings. This is essential to aid processing and to facilitate movement between emotions. It also aids understanding and is a tool that can aid the monitoring of mental health.

7. **Independence** – The capacity to work or play alone promotes self-sufficiency, contentment and confidence. Utilising one's own resources to achieve a task is an important developmental skill. It can be experienced and promoted in all tasks, including computer gaming. Independence suggests a security and belief in one's own capacity to get on, as well as the ability to seek support if or when required.

Compassion

The assessment theme of compassion encourages consideration of the pupil's strengths and barriers in relation to:

1. **Friendships** – Initiating and sustaining friendships over time requires the application of many social communication and social interaction skills. It also requires acceptance, trust and often involves turn taking and shared interests. Sustaining friendships involves the management and resolution of conflicts and an ability to share and support others. When evaluating this aspect, it may be useful to consider these questions:
   - Is the child or young person able to initiate and sustain positive relationships with peers over time?
   - How stable are friendships?
   - How do they respond and manage conflict?

2. **Turn-taking** – This skill explores an individual's ability to wait and to turn take. It involves self-regulation and the control of impulsivity, and a willingness to share. When evaluating this theme, it may be useful to consider these questions:
   - Is the learner able to hold their ideas and control the impulsive desire to blurt out or interrupt?
   - Are they able to share resources, friendships, personal space?
   - Do they watch and listen while the other person has their turn?

3. **Empathy** – The skill of empathy is the insightful anticipation of the experiences of others – being able to consider the views from another perspective. It requires understanding, compassion and care. A learner may reveal empathy if they are able to consider what an incident or event may feel like to someone else, even if they have not directly felt the same thing.

4. **Sense of Justice** – This attribute relates to the development of one's own ethical code, including a clear sense of right and wrong. It promotes a social conscience and an understanding of consequences. It could include a passion for the environment and a love of nature.

5. **Self-esteem** – This relates to a feeling or sense of self-worth and a belief in one's own value and contribution. A learner may present with inflated or deflated esteem, both of which can be limiting. Acquiring a positive sense of worth and relevance whilst avoiding self-inflated importance or the active devaluing of

others is a tremendous strength. When evaluating this skill, it may be useful to consider the following questions:

- Does the child or young person feel valued and worthy?
- Do they magnify their own importance or seek to put down others?
- Can they identify strengths and successes, or do they continue to seek assurance from others?

6. **Self-efficacy** – Self-efficacy relates to whether a learner believes they can 'effect' change. It is their sense of impact and contribution or whether they perceive that they 'matter'. A high sense of self-efficacy is the opposite of 'learned helplessness', meaning a learner believes they have the capacity to make a difference and it would matter if they were not there. When considering this skill, these questions may be useful:

- How effective does the learner believe they are?
- Can they shape, influence or change outcomes by their actions?
- Does anything they do, actually make a difference or a contribution for themselves or for others?

7. **Support for Others** – This attribute encourages consideration regarding the capacity of one child to befriend and encourage another child. There are children who are always 'chosen' to be the one who 'helps' or models expected behaviour for another child. Or they offer unprompted care and compassion to support a peer when they are feeling sad, isolated or afraid.

Co-ordination

Within the assessment theme of co-ordination, consideration is given to the pupil's strengths and barriers relating to:

1. **Fine Motor skills** – These relate to the fluency and accuracy of the distal muscles and finger control, used for handwriting, cutting, threading, weaving and other such activities requiring the manipulation of fingers or fine motor movements. This control enables the completion of smaller or fine motor skills.

2. **Gross Motor skills** – These relate to the fluency and accuracy of larger movements including running, walking, jumping, hopping, skipping and control with kicking, catching, rolling and throwing a ball. The connection of these movements is also significant in terms of overall co-ordination. Is the child able to

run and kick a ball? Hop, skip and jump? Or combine with other objects, such as riding a bike or using a trampoline?

3. **Sensory** – This relates to the experience and application of the senses, including the five senses of vision, hearing, touch, taste and smell plus the further two senses of proprioception (knowledge of our own body in space) and vestibular sense (balance.) When considering this, it is useful to notice if the child accesses information from each sense in the same way as others, or if there is any dominance, preference or difficulty. It is useful to seek additional assessment or checks of sensory information (such as an eye or hearing check) if there are emerging concerns.

4. **Mobility** – This relates to ease of movement and effective transitioning across space. Consideration should be given to whether the learner is able to walk, stand or run or whether they need to use aids to assist with movements. Useful questions include:
   - How mobile is the child or young person?
   - Are they able to stand, walk, run?
   - Do they have an expected walking gait or are there alignment issues?
   - Can they move independently with or without a mobility aid?
   - Are they able to explore the environment and interact with others, or is a mobility aid a 'barrier' to engagement due to a difference in height or speed?

5. **Stability and Balance** – Consider the fluency and accuracy and control that the child or young person has over their movements. Observe whether they find running easier than walking, as this could suggest that they find it harder to 'stop' and control the physical movement. Notice their response to spinning and whether they regularly fall, trip or stand on others.

6. **Posture** – Consider the preferred positioning of the child or young person and whether they able to sit up straight on a chair with their feet on the floor. Ensure that furniture is the right height for them and notice whether they rock or swing on the furniture or regularly change posture. Observe the application of core muscles in relation to the adoption of a working posture.

7. **Sensory Processing** – This skill relates to an ability to filter, respond or extract sensory information. Look for evidence of any heightened sensitivity to certain types of sensory information (hyper-response), for example, covering their ears to avoid loud or unexpected sounds, covering their eyes when the lights are on, or flinching when touched. Similarly, look for evidence of under-

sensitivity (hypo-response), where the learner will seek sensory information, such as shouting, pressing hard, squeezing hard, seeking bright lights etc. It is essential that observations are shared with the parents/carers to consider if they are also present in other contexts. If there are concerns, it may be useful to seek additional assessment or advice.

Curriculum

This assessment theme is likely to feel the most familiar. Indeed, you may choose to personalise this section, preferring to use your own language or systems for curriculum assessment including for example, modern foreign languages or other subjects you teach that are not referenced here. As with all information in this book, this is offered as a starting point to facilitate discussion and thinking and not as a definitive model or checklist. As a starting point you may wish to consider the child or young person's strengths and barriers in relation to:

1. **English** – Consider the learner's acquired skills in relation to reading, writing and spelling and whether they are able to use and apply these skills in a range of contexts. It may be useful to consider these questions:
   - Can the learner read, write and spell independently and at expected levels for their age?
   - What are their levels of fluency and accuracy as well as confidence and presentation?
   - Do they understand phonics and phonological awareness and have a developing sight vocabulary?

2. **Maths** – Consider the acquisition and application of skills relating to number, shape, measurement, time, money and whether they are able to recall and apply prior subject knowledge. It may be useful to consider these questions:
   - Does the learner understand number value and have fluency and accuracy with addition, subtraction, multiplication and division?
   - Can they apply these skills to money and time?
   - Can they access the language of maths, recognising more and less than, big and small and do they have an awareness of shape and space?

3. **Science** – Consider the skills and knowledge acquired in relation to science concepts and tools. Evaluate skills of investigation, prediction, recording and summarising information. It may be useful to consider these questions:
   - How confident is the learner in exploring stimuli, monitoring changes applying a methodical structure of evaluation?

- Do they ask questions and challenge answers?
- Can they identify similarities and differences and group and categorise?
- Are they curious about the world around them and how and where they fit in?

4. **Art and Music** – This attribute encourages consideration of the learner's understanding and interest in exploring a range of materials and sounds as an expression of thoughts, feelings and imagery, in addition to their understanding and skills with each subject area. For example:
   - Is the learner able to utilise equipment (musical instruments or art materials) to replicate, create and express sounds or images?
   - How do they respond to music and art works?
   - Are they able to express likes and dislikes across subjects?

5. **History and Geography** – This aspect of learning looks for evidence of strengths and/or areas for development in relation to understanding time and historical events, as well as the world around them. It may be useful to consider the following questions:
   - Can the learner describe, interpret and evaluate events from the past and assimilate knowledge of their present?
   - Are they aware of their environment, location, weather and position in the world?
   - What skills have they developed to aid analysis, reflection and evaluation of historical events and/or geographical and environmental realities?

6. **Computing** – This attribute relates to the knowledge, confidence and experience with the application of IT including computer programming, software application and gaming. It may be useful to consider:
   - How confident is the learner to engage with technology utilising and programming equipment to achieve specific outcomes?
   - How fluent and accurate is their understanding of the language of IT and its evolutionary role?
   - Are they able to maximise the potential of IT resources to help them to achieve specific outcomes?

7. **PE and Sport** – This theme encourages consideration of fitness, physical and mental health and well being as well as co-ordinated action within structured team games or individual activities. It may be useful to consider the following questions:
   - Can the learner understand and follow specific rules in games and sports?

- Do they demonstrate fair play and can they respond and manage emotions linked to winning and losing?
- What types of activities or sports are strengths and/or require development?

Implications for SENCOs and SEN Practitioners

The 7 Cs Learning Portfolio seeks to provide a language of assessment that includes but goes beyond a subject curriculum. It is intended to encourage learning conversations with learners and their families. The 7 Cs Learning Portfolio provides a language which helps to assess barriers to learning and identify and value existing strengths which could be utilised to overcome or where possible remove barriers to learning. For example, if assessment using the 7 Cs Learning Portfolio suggests that a learner has excellent social communication and interaction skills and is a great friend and supporter of others, it may be appropriate to use a peer mentor or collaborative learning approach, as part of an intervention to aid the development of their reading skills, thus, using their strengths to help improve areas of development. **Sharing a language of assessment that is additional to and different from the curriculum assessment (which should be going on anyway) helps to inform the identification of provision that is additional to or different from the differentiated curriculum.** In the next chapter the options for using and applying the 7 Cs Learning Portfolio will be explored.

Reflections...

- What are the strengths of the 7 Cs Learning Portfolio?
- Could this help to structure a shared language of assessment in your school or setting?
- Are you already using something similar that could assimilate this approach?

References

Bouncing Back & Coping with Change: Building Emotional & Social Resilience in Young People Aged 9–14 (2016) Tina Rae. Buckingham: Hinton House Publishers.

Special Educational Needs and Disability Code of Practice: 0 to 25 Years – Statutory Guidance for Organisations which Work with and Support Children and Young People who have Special Educational Needs or Disabilities (2014; updated 2015). Department for Education and Department of Health.

Working Memory and Learning: A Practical Guide for Teachers (2008) Susan Gathercole and Tracy Packiam Alloway. London: Paul Chapman Publishing.

6. Using the 7 Cs Learning Portfolio

The 7 Cs Learning Portfolio has four possible applications. The first three options for application, 'functional', 'intermediate' and 'extensive' referenced in chapter 5, will be described in detail in this chapter, but the fourth cannot be described beyond two words: 'your way!' You may read these three 'models' and create your own application, which is great. You are of course asked to acknowledge the origins of the work to the 7 Cs Learning Portfolio and this book, but beyond that, please modify as appears most relevant to your staff and setting.

The 'functional' application of the 7 Cs Learning Portfolio

This approach is the least time-consuming model and can be integrated into existing school or setting systems. It simply involves sharing the 7 Cs Learning Portfolio with staff or using it as the SENCO or SEN Practitioner to inform your language of assessment. The 7 Cs Learning Portfolio has been summarised on to a single sheet of A4, which can be folded to create a pocket-sized booklet. Those of you familiar with creating such books will know that it is all about the accuracy of folding! Fold the sheet in half and then fold each page. Open it up and then cut along the blue line. Use this cut to concertina the pages open and then fold. (It is far easier to do than to describe and if in doubt look on YouTube or ask a 7-year-old, as they always appear to 'know' these things!)

7 Cs Learning Portfolio

Cognition
- Working Memory
- Speed of Processing
- Inference
- Anticipation
- Reflection
- Evaluation
- Analysis

Communication
- Speech - Expressive Vocab
  - Articulation
- Language - Understanding Vocab
- Collaborative Conversation
- Listening - Follow Instructions
- Social Communication(Output)
- Social Interaction(Input)

Curriculum
- English ⋏ Reading
  ⋏ Writing
  ⋏ Spelling
- Math ⋏ Number
  ⋏ Shape/Space
- Science
- Art & Music
- History & Geography
- Computing
- PE & Sport

Co-ordination
- Fine Motor - Handwriting, Cutting, Threading
- Gross Motor- Jumping, Hopping, Kick, Catch, Throw a Ball
- Sensory – vision, hearing, tracking
- Mobility
- Stability + Balance
- Posture
- Sensory Processing

Creativity
- Generate Ideas
- Problem Solving
- Attention
- Motivation
- Making Things
- Courage-Determination
- Trust

Control
- Self Regulation
- Behaviour for Learning
- Anxiety Management
- Confidence
- Resilience
- Language of Emotions
- Independence

Compassion
- Friendships
- Turn Taking
- Empathy
- Sense of Justice
- Self Esteem & Wellbeing
- Self Efficacy
- Support for Others

COMPANION @ WEBSITE

The purpose of the booklet is to remind you of the themes and to promote a discussion about strengths and barriers to learning. The booklet itself is not intended to be written on, but it can act as a useful prompt to help structure existing SEN Support review meetings. You can identify the three strengths and three areas for development and record these in your existing SEN Support paperwork. For example, if you use learning passports, individual learning plans or 'about me' forms, the language can be integrated into your existing systems.

As previously mentioned, this is the 'light touch' approach and a very useful starting point. Staff simply need an opportunity to be informed of the rationale of a strengths-based approach to SEN assessment and to listen to and understand the content and 49 descriptors in the 7 Cs Learning Portfolio. The disadvantage of only using this approach is that the learner and their family may not have an opportunity to share this language of assessment, so you may not be maximising the full potential of the approach, as in many ways the assessment conversation is still being done 'to' the learner and their family, rather than 'with' them. That said you could share the 7 Cs Learning Portfolio User Guide with the learner and their family (detailed in the 'extensive' approach and included at the end of this chapter) which may mitigate this risk as over time, all participants would share the same language of assessment.

The 'intermediate' application of the 7 Cs Learning Portfolio

The intermediate application extends the functional approach further, as it includes bespoke action planning record forms. The intention is that these would be adapted to become the SEN Support record (or assess, plan, do are review format) used at the school or setting, thus reducing the risk of duplication or additional paperwork. All participants would need to have an understanding of the shared language of the 7 Cs Learning Portfolio (using the A4 booklet and user guide) but the three strengths and three areas for development would be recorded on either the action plan or the learner leaflet (presented at the end of this chapter.) These would then be reviewed as a review of SEN Support.

Adopting the bespoke paperwork can help to reinforce the use of the shared language, as it increases familiarity and experience with the language. It also promotes consistency, which in turn may support your monitoring of the system. Two recording examples are provided at the end of the chapter, but of course, you may decide to modify these, combining them with your existing formats and then adopting this version for use at SEN Support meetings.

The 'extensive' application of the 7 Cs Learning Portfolio

The extensive approach is aptly named, as it involves fully embedding the language of the 7 Cs Learning Portfolio amongst all staff and the learners and their families who will be using the portfolio. This could be with a particular group of pupils, such as those at SEN Support, or it could be a tool to aid learning for everyone! (That truly is extensive.) As before, it is essential that staff know and understand the rationale of using a strengths–based approach to assessment and feel confident and comfortable with the language of the 7 Cs Learning Portfolio. (This in itself, may trigger additional CPD needs for staff such as on Working Memory, Social Communication or Speech and Language, as staff may request additional information or resources about these attributes.) It is also important that learners and their families are empowered to have the same access to the shared language of the 7 Cs Learning Portfolio via the user guide. The extensive model of application requires that each learner using the 7 Cs Learning Portfolio has a printed or electronic copy of the user guide at the start of an academic year. This is personalised by them and completed at different stages during the year as part of a learning conversation or SEN Support review meeting. How this is completed is optional. It could be that the learner and their parents/carers choose to read the whole document together over time and the learner baselines their perceived scores for each area. This is used by the learner to then identify three strengths and three areas for development to be worked on during that term or half-term. Alternatively, the teacher may 'chunk' individual 'Cs' and ask the learner and family to focus on specific areas. Or it may be that the user guide is used for reference and as a prompt to identify three strengths and three areas for development. There really is not a 'right' or 'wrong' way of application; furthermore, it can be applied differently according to learner, family and teacher need or preference. And of course, there is the fourth model of application which is 'your way'. So perhaps you are already developing your thoughts about how this could be most effective in your setting? Keep thinking as you read the following set of materials and examples.

Learning Portfolio Priority Action Sheet

Name: Joanne Harford   **School:** Willow Tree School   **Date Completed:** 22-10-20
Completed by: Mr Jones (SENCO) Miss Leitz (C/T) Ms Harford and Jo

We have identified many learning strengths for Joanne including these:
1. **COMPASSION: Friendships** – Jo is a lovely friend and is a popular member of class
2. **CONTROL: Language of emotions** – Jo is able to talk about her feelings at home and school
3. **CO-ORDINATION – Fine motor skills** – Jo is able to write neatly and enjoys craft activities

We have agreed that the 3 actions to be worked on this half term are:
1. **COGNITION – Working memory** – we want Jo to try to hold more verbal information
2. **CURRICULUM – Reading** – Jo can read 12 letter sounds and we want her to read 20
3. **CONTROL – Anxiety management** – we want Jo to feel more confident when Mum leaves her at school

To help develop these skills in school we will:
1. **COGNITION – Working memory** – we will play verbal memory games and rehearse 2, 3 & 4 digits forwards & backwards
2. **CURRICULUM – Reading** – Jo will work with the TA twice a day to rehearse the 12 letter sounds she knows plus 8 new sounds, using direct instruction and interleaved learning
3. **CONTROL – Anxiety management** – Jo will set up a crafts club before school and invite some other peers to attend. Mum will drop her off at the class door.

At home we will:
1. **COGNITION – Working memory** – we will play verbal memory games such as I went shopping and will ask Jo to collect items from different rooms in the house or to collect items from the supermarket shelves when shopping.
2. **CURRICULUM – Reading** – Jo's 20 letters will be put on the fridge door and her bedroom door at home and she will read them out with Mum every day.
3. **CONTROL – Anxiety management** –Talk about the craft activity Jo will be doing at her club and agree what Jo will do at the club so she will be able to show Mum at the end of the day.

As a result, we anticipate that Joanne will be able to:
1. **COGNITION – Working memory** – Recall 3 part verbal instructions
2. **CURRICULUM – Reading** – Read 20 letter sounds
3. **CONTROL – Anxiety management** – Positively separate from Mum in the mornings.

  Willow Tree Learning 2021

Learning Portfolio Priority Action Sheet

Pupil Name: **School:**   **Date Completed**

Completed by whom:

We have identified many learning strengths including these 3:

1.

2.

3.

We have agreed that the 3 actions to be worked on this half term are:

1.

2.

3.

To help develop these skills in school we will:

1.

2.

3.

At home we will:

1.

2.

3.

As a result, we anticipate that ……….will be able to:

1.

2.

3.

We will meet to review this on:

The 7 Cs Learning Portfolio – Action Plan

Name: Jasmine Khan

School: Willow Academy

Birthday: 8-12-13

Date completed: 15-1-20

Written by: Ms Carter, Jasmine and Mrs Khan (Mum)

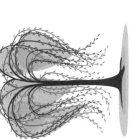

My Next Steps...

We will meet again on:
14th February 2020

My Review

How did I get on?

1.

My rating scale today is...

1 2 3 4 5 6 7 8 9 10

2.

My rating scale today is...

1 2 3 4 5 6 7 8 9 10

3.

My rating scale today is...

1 2 3 4 5 6 7 8 9 10

About Me…

Things I like:
Playing Minecraft and colouring

What I find tricky:
Reading and maths

I'm good at: *drawing and playing with my friends*

I'd like to be good at: *maths and reading*

What people like about me:
I am funny and caring and I help people.

My Strengths…

We have identified many learning strengths including these:

1. *Compassion: Friendships*
   1 2 3 4 5 6 7 (8) 9 10

2. *Compassion: Support for Others*
   1 2 3 4 5 6 7 (8) 9 10

3. *Coordination: Fine Motor Skills*
   1 2 3 4 5 6 (7) 8 9 10

My 3 Actions to work on are…

1. **Cognition: Working Memory**
   My rating scale today is…
   1 2 3 (4) 5 6 7 8 9 10

2. *Cognition: Inference*
   My rating scale today is…
   1 2 (3) 4 5 6 7 8 9 10

3. *Curriculum: Maths*
   My rating scale today is…
   1 2 3 4 (5) 6 7 8 9 10

To help develop these skills in school I will:

1. *Join the memory club and play games twice a week for 4 weeks.*

2. *Group reading 3 times a week where I will be asked to stop and think about the story….*

3. *Use cubes to help me add on and take away numbers up to 25*

At home or when I'm out and about I will…

1. *Try to remember and collect 2 items from the shopping list*

2. *Watch a TV programme with Mum or Dad and pause it to think about what might happen next*

3. *Share out grapes with my brothers, counting out fairly*

By doing this, we hope I will be able to…

1. *Remember 2-or 3-part instructions and find ways to help me remember*

2. *Think ahead and predict what might happen next*

3. *Confidently add and takeaway up to 25*

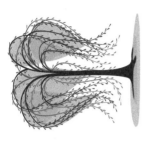

The 7 Cs Learning Portfolio – Action Plan

Name:

School:

Birthday:

Date completed:

Written by:

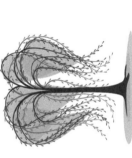

My Next Steps...

We will meet again on:

My Review

How did I get on?

1.

My rating scale today is...

1   2   3   4   5   6   7   8   9   10

2.

My rating scale today is...

1   2   3   4   5   6   7   8   9   10

3.

My rating scale today is...

1   2   3   4   5   6   7   8   9   10

About Me…

Things I like:

What I find tricky:

I'm good at:

I'd like to be good at:

What people like about me:

My Strengths…

We have identified many learning strengths including these:

1.
1 2 3 4 5 6 7 8 9 10

2.
1 2 3 4 5 6 7 8 9 10

3.
1 2 3 4 5 6 7 8 9 10

My 3 Actions to work on are…

1.
My rating scale today is…
1 2 3 4 5 6 7 8 9 10

2.
My rating scale today is…
1 2 3 4 5 6 7 8 9 10

3.
My rating scale today is…
1 2 3 4 5 6 7 8 9 10

To help develop these skills in school I will:

1.

2.

3.

At home or when I'm out and about I will…

1.

2.

3.

By doing this, we hope I will be able to…

1.

2.

3.

© Willow Tree Learning Ltd 2021

COMPANION @ WEBSITE

My 7 Cs Learning Portfolio

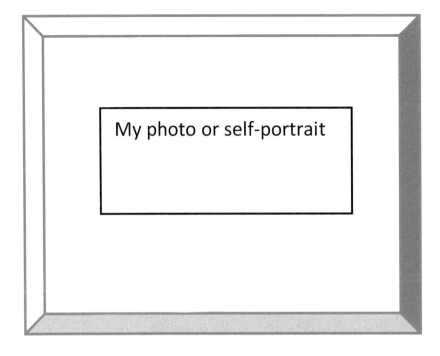

My photo or self-portrait

Name:

Age:

School:

Year group:

Date completed:

Date of 1st review:

Date of 2nd review:

Date of 3rd review:

The 7 Cs Learning Portfolio has been written to help you and the adults that work with you, to name the things that you are good at as a learner (your strengths), and the things you would like to be good at (your developments). It has 7 themes, which all begin with the letter C! With an adult, take a look at each of the 7 Cs and talk about these and agree 3 strengths and 3 developments. You can then agree what might help you to achieve your next learning steps.

 Willow Tree Learning 2021

Cognition

Cognition is the first C and it means thinking. What are your thinking strengths and areas for development? Read each of the following and consider your skills. What mark out of 10 would you give yourself if 10 was the very best mark and 1 the lowest?

Working Memory is what I use to 'hold' information before I remember it in my long-term memory. So if someone at home asks me to go and get my shoes, bag and jumper, do I remember this or do I end up in my room and have to ask what am I supposed to be getting? Also do I listen to the Teacher but when we are told to start work, have no idea what I should be doing?

1	2	3	4	5	6	7	8	9	10

Speed of Processing is how quickly I can take on information and keep up with others. Do I find myself feeling confused in class and wishing the Teacher would slow down? Is it hard to follow what is being said?

1	2	3	4	5	6	7	8	9	10

Inference is what I make if I listen and use key bits of information to make a prediction or guess. When I'm reading or listening can I imagine what might happen next or what it would be like if that happened to me? Can I work out what I should do next from listening to part of the instruction?

1	2	3	4	5	6	7	8	9	10

Anticipation is what I do when I stop, think and consider what might happen next.

Am I able to pause and consider what might happen if... or do I tend to rush ahead? This can be with work or with other things. Can I use the information I have to work out what I might need to do next or do I always ask someone?

1	2	3	4	5	6	7	8	9	10

Reflection is when I think back over something that has happened.

Am I reflective? Will I consider what has happened and whether I can learn from this? Or do I just move on and not review or think back?

1	2	3	4	5	6	7	8	9	10

Evaluation is when I think about something and weigh it up, deciding whether it was good or bad.

Am I able to consider the pros and cons, advantages and disadvantages and then make a judgement for myself? Can I capture this 'weighing up' process in my work?

1	2	3	4	5	6	7	8	9	10

Analysis is when I focus on something and consider it against something else and make a decision about it.

Do I consider options or actions and consider whether they are useful or not? Do I focus on details and look at how they are like each other or how they are different?

1	2	3	4	5	6	7	8	9	10

*Did you choose any strengths or developments from **Cognition?** Keep going and think about the next C which is **communication**.*

Willow Tree Learning 2021

Communication

Communication is how we talk, listen and understand each other. These skills include:

Expressive Vocabulary, which is my 'pool' or amount of words that I can say.

Do I sometimes feel frustrated because I can't think of the word I want to say? Do I find it easier to describe things and wait for someone else to tell me the word?

1	2	3	4	5	6	7	8	9	10

Articulation is how I say words and sounds.

Are there any words or sounds I find it hard to say? Do I stumble over saying some sounds or words?

1	2	3	4	5	6	7	8	9	10

Language and Comprehension describes the words that I understand and know the meaning of.

Do I understand the words that people say, or do I find that I understand some of what they say, so I then try to guess the rest? Do I read words in books but not know what they mean?

1	2	3	4	5	6	7	8	9	10

Collaborative Conversation is the way that I talk and listen to other people.

Do I take part in a conversation where I say something and listen to what the other person says next? Or do I tend to talk 'at' people just saying what I think and not really listening to what they say?

1	2	3	4	5	6	7	8	9	10

Listening is when I can focus on what has been said and respond to it.

Do I listen or does my mind wander on to other things when people are talking? Do I tend to talk more than listen, so I 'miss' what people are actually saying to me?

1	2	3	4	5	6	7	8	9	10

Social Communication is the skills I use when I am with people, including whether I look at them, talk to them and give them time to talk.

How do I feel in social situations? Am I ok or do I feel nervous or excited? Do I talk at people or pretend that they are not there and carry on with my own thing? Do I let other people talk or do I just say what I think of when I think of it?

1	2	3	4	5	6	7	8	9	10

Social Interaction is the skills I use when people are with me, including whether I know how to respond to what they say or do.

Do I want people to act in the way I think they will? If they do something I didn't think they would do, does it make me feel worried, confused, angry or am I ok with it? If I'm not sure what to do, will I ask them what they mean or just ignore them and get on with what I was doing?

1	2	3	4	5	6	7	8	9	10

*Did you choose any strengths or developments from **Communication?** Keep going and think about the next C which is **creativity**.*

Willow Tree Learning 2021

Creativity

Creativity is about how I think and whether I can build, make or do something.

Generation of ideas is my skill of thinking of new things and making suggestions.

Is it easy for me to think of lots of new ideas? Do I always make suggestions and am I keen to share them?

1	2	3	4	5	6	7	8	9	10

Problem-solving is when I think of what I know and how to use it to overcome a problem.

If there is a problem am I able to solve it on my own? Do I have a go even if I'm wrong or will I avoid it, ask for help or see what everyone else does? Am I able to use what I already know to help me?

1	2	3	4	5	6	7	8	9	10

Attention is how I focus and concentrate on something.

Do I stay focused or do I get distracted? Is it hard for me to stay focused on the one thing as I notice everything else that is going on around me? Can I concentrate until a job is done or do I end up doing something else?

1	2	3	4	5	6	7	8	9	10

Motivation is whether I want to do something or not.

Do I like what I'm doing and do I want to keep doing it until it is done? If I start to lose focus can I refocus myself as I really want to succeed and finish the task?

1	2	3	4	5	6	7	8	9	10

Making Things is my skill of building, designing and creating. It could be on the computer, using junk, bricks, craft paper or anything!

Am I good at building and construction or craft and design? Do I like Lego, models, sewing, crafting, junk modelling, Minecraft, sculpture, pottery or other such things? Can I work out how things go and stay together?

1	2	3	4	5	6	7	8	9	10

Courage and Determination is about whether I am brave to have a go at something and whether I 'stick with it' even if it gets tricky.

How do I feel when I am asked to do something that is tricky, challenging or scary? Do I want to give up in case I'm wrong, or am I brave and will try and do my best? Will I keep going even if I feel confused just because I really want to find out how to do it?

1	2	3	4	5	6	7	8	9	10

Trust is believing in someone or something enough, so I will take a 'risk.'

Do I believe people around me or do I feel a little uncertain? If I feel unsure or insecure is it harder for me to do something just because someone told me to? Or do I believe that people want the best for me so it is OK to try?

1	2	3	4	5	6	7	8	9	10

*Did you choose any strengths or developments from **Creativity?** Keep going and think about the next C which is **control**.*

Willow Tree Learning 2021

Control

Control is about how I manage myself. These skills include:

Self-regulation is whether I can stay in control of my words, feelings and actions in different situations.

Do I get cross or upset really quickly? Can I end up losing control of my words, feelings and actions because of something or someone? When I get angry or upset is it hard for me to calm myself down quickly? Or am I able to stay in control and talk about my feelings at another time?

1	2	3	4	5	6	7	8	9	10

Behaviour for learning is whether I am 'ready' to listen, learn and take part in lessons and activities.

Am I able to get on at school and show that I am listening and ready to learn? Can I get the equipment I need to start work or does it take me a while? Do I take a long time to start work?

1	2	3	4	5	6	7	8	9	10

Anxiety Management is whether I can control my feelings or worries and fears.

When I feel worried or frightened am I able to 'notice' this but carry on anyway, or do I feel upset and unable to carry on? Do I lose control of my feelings and become angry or scared and I either hit out at people or want to hide away?

1	2	3	4	5	6	7	8	9	10

Confidence is whether I believe in myself and my skills.

Do I think I can have a go at most things, even if I find them tricky, or do I doubt myself and my skills and think that everyone else could do better than me? Am I proud of who I am and what I can do or do I wish I could be someone else and do other things?

| 1 | 2 | 3 | 4 | 5 | 6 | 7 | 8 | 9 | 10 |

Resilience is the likelihood that I will 'bounce back' and keep going even when things go wrong.

When something goes wrong what do I do and feel? Do I want to hide away and never do that again? Or will I have another go and try again knowing that I still might not be able to do it, but I might get a bit further? Will I try and try again?

| 1 | 2 | 3 | 4 | 5 | 6 | 7 | 8 | 9 | 10 |

Language of Emotions is whether I can use words to talk about my feelings and can express my physical and mental health needs and wellbeing.

Am I able to talk about how I feel or do I tend to show my feelings by my actions? Do I know when I feel physically unwell or hurt myself and when my feelings feel hurt or confusing? Can I tell people this with words and ask for help?

| 1 | 2 | 3 | 4 | 5 | 6 | 7 | 8 | 9 | 10 |

Independence is my skill of working, playing or being on my own.

What am I like on my own? Do I have the skills and resources I need to get on or do I prefer to work or be with other people because I'm not sure I do have the skills and resources I need? If I am on my own do I get on with what I have been asked to do, or do I distract myself and find something else to do?

| 1 | 2 | 3 | 4 | 5 | 6 | 7 | 8 | 9 | 10 |

Did you choose any strengths or developments from **Control?** *Keep going and think about the next C which is* **Compassion**.

Willow Tree Learning 2021

Compassion

Compassion is about the skills I use to show my feelings, to show how I care and how I am with other people. They include:

Friendships are the positive relationships I make with others so whether I have friends and or am a good friend.

Do I make friends easily? If I have friends are we always falling out and arguing or do we work out our difficulties? Would I like to have (more) friends but am not sure how to make friends? Do I think other people like me and do I like other people? Or am I a friend that others want to have?

1	2	3	4	5	6	7	8	9	10

Turn-taking is whether I can follow rules and 'wait' or if I interrupt or call out without waiting.

Do I take turns or do I tend to call out or try and jump ahead so it is my turn again? Am I good at waiting or do I get too excited and just want to have my go?

1	2	3	4	5	6	7	8	9	10

Empathy is when I show an understanding of what someone else might be feeling even if I am not feeling the same way.

Can I understand how someone else might feel in a situation and do I try to show that understanding to them? Am I able to imagine what it might be like to be them and does this help me to help them?

1	2	3	4	5	6	7	8	9	10

Sense of Justice is whether I believe in 'right and wrong' for myself and others.

Do I have a clear sense of what is 'fair' and what is 'right' and 'wrong?' Do I try and stand up for other people to ensure that they are treated fairly? Or do I tend to do my own thing?

1	2	3	4	5	6	7	8	9	10

Self-esteem is whether I think I have 'value' and am aware of myself and my mental health.

Do I think that I am as important as other people, or do I think I am more or less important? Do I think I am valued by other people and I am aware of my own sense of self, well being and happiness?

1	2	3	4	5	6	7	8	9	10

Self-efficacy is if I believe that I can make a difference for myself or that my views matter.

Do I think that what I do makes a difference? Can I make a difference? Do people 'notice' if I am there or not? Can I make choices and decisions that will make a difference? Am I as important and 'powerful' as other people?

1	2	3	4	5	6	7	8	9	10

Support for Others is whether I help other people.

Am I kind and considerate to others and do I try to help them? Am I asked to be a friend or helper to someone or do I tend to look after myself and not always 'notice' what other people need?

1	2	3	4	5	6	7	8	9	10

Did you choose any strengths or developments from **Compassion?** *Keep going and think about the next C which is* **Co-ordination**.

Willow Tree Learning 2021

Co-ordination

Co-ordination is about how I control and organise things including my body. Think about these:

Fine Motor skills are used to control small movements such as hand movements when playing computer games, cutting and writing.

Can I control my writing, drawing, cutting and painting? Can I use these skills quickly but still do them neatly and carefully or do I need a long time to do them and even then, it is not always clear what I have done? Do I have good hand eye co-ordination when using a games controller?

1	2	3	4	5	6	7	8	9	10

Gross Motor skills are used to control large movements such as walking, running, jumping, kicking and throwing.

How controlled are my movements when I walk, run, jump, hop and skip? Can I catch, throw and kick a ball or do I tend to go off target a little? Am I a bit clumsy or need a bit of help?

1	2	3	4	5	6	7	8	9	10

Sensory skills are how I use my senses to gain information, so how I see, hear, smell, taste and touch.

Am I able to see, hear, smell, taste and touch things? Do I do any of these things more or less than other people? Do I like and use one of these more than the others?

1	2	3	4	5	6	7	8	9	10

Mobility skills are how I move around.

Am I able to walk, stand and run on my own? Does it take me a bit longer than other people? Am I faster than other people or about the same? Do I need any aids to help me get around? Can I use these on my own or do I need help?

1	2	3	4	5	6	7	8	9	10

Stability and Balance is how controlled I am when moving and whether I am likely to fall over.

Do I have good balance when I am sitting, standing or running? Do I fall over a lot or about the same as other people? Do I need any aids to help me?

1	2	3	4	5	6	7	8	9	10

Posture is how I sit and stand and whether I lean over a lot or slouch.

Is it comfortable when I sit or stand up straight? Can I stay in the same position or do I move around a lot and fidget? Do I lean on people or objects or do I stay sitting or standing straight on my own?

1	2	3	4	5	6	7	8	9	10

Sensory Processing is how I experience and respond to information from my senses.

Do I complain that noises are too loud or do I like to make lots of noise? Do I like bright lights or colours or find they hurt my eyes? Do I tend to bite my pencil or chew my sleeves or hair? Do I like to lick or taste objects and do I hate or like being hugged? Am I too aware of somethings or not aware enough of others?

1	2	3	4	5	6	7	8	9	10

*Did you choose any strengths or developments from **Co-ordination?** Keep going and think about the next C which is **Curriculum**.*

Willow Tree Learning 2021

Curriculum

Curriculum skills are the skills and knowledge I have gained from learning subjects and topics taught to me. Think about these:

English includes my skills with reading, writing and spelling.

How do I get on with reading, writing and spelling? Do I find any or all of these a bit tricky or am I good at any or all of these? Has that always been the case?

1	2	3	4	5	6	7	8	9	10

Maths are my skills with number, value, shapes, fractions, money, time and other things.

How do I get on with Maths? Is any part of maths easy, difficult or just ok? Does it help if I can use counters or write things down? Do I find it takes a while to learn something new but when I get it, I get it, or is it really easy or does it feel really tricky?

1	2	3	4	5	6	7	8	9	10

Science skills are the skills I use to explore, predict, test, make connections and understand the world around me and how it works.

Do I like Science? What do I remember learning about? Do I like experiments and practical work or watching, reading and listening about science information?

1	2	3	4	5	6	7	8	9	10

Art and Music are my skills with creative works and my experience of music and instruments.

Do I think I am artistic and or musical? Do I like listening to music, learning about music and or playing instruments and singing? Do I like painting, drawing, printing, collaging, sculpting and looking at art work?

1	2	3	4	5	6	7	8	9	10

History and Geography are my skills and knowledge with events in the past and understanding of the Earth.

Am I good at history and learning about events from the past or do I find it a bit confusing? What about geography? Do I like learning about the world, rivers, oceans, the weather, rocks and understanding how it all works together or is it not for me?

1	2	3	4	5	6	7	8	9	10

Computing is my skills with programming and using IT tools and applications to do tasks.

Do I think I am good with computers? Can I programme and use the apps on a tablet, phone or laptop? Can I type, voice record or use a camera to capture ideas and edit them? Am I a gamer who is skilled at playing computer games?

1	2	3	4	5	6	7	8	9	10

PE and Sport are about my skills and knowledge of fitness, sports, physical and mental health.

Do I have a favourite sport that I like to watch and play? Do I like team games or solo sports? Am I aware of my health and fitness and do I enjoy learning new activities and skills? Do I feel healthier from sports?

1	2	3	4	5	6	7	8	9	10

*Did you choose any strengths or developments from **Curriculum? Congratulations, you have completed the 7 Cs learning assessment and now have at least 3 strengths and 3 areas to develop. Perhaps you can start to think about how you can use your strengths to help you develop other skills? Good luck and keep working hard!***

Willow Tree Learning 2021

My 3 strengths are:

1.

2.

3.

My 3 areas to develop are:

1.

2.

3.

What I will do at school to develop these skills:

1.

2.

3.

What I will do at home:

1.

2.

3.

What I will do when I am out and about:

1.

2.

3.

How did I get on?   What's next?

Implications for SENCOs and SEN Practitioners

The ultimate implication of this chapter is for you to decide whether you like the language of the 7 Cs Learning Portfolio and if yes, how you can share this with staff, learners and families. If you don't like the 7 Cs Learning Portfolio, the content of the book so far may have inspired you to consider how you can develop your own shared language of SEN assessment that includes but also exceeds curriculum subjects. If that is the case, do advance your thinking with this and develop your own approach so you can be sure that barriers to learning are not identified only by performance in curriculum subjects. However, if you do like the rationale of adopting a strengths-based approach to assessment and you like the shared language of the 7 Cs Learning Portfolio, the following questions may be useful to help advance your application of this:

- What did you like about this?
- What do you think would be different if you adopted this approach?
- How do you think staff will respond to this?
- What opportunities could you have to share this with staff? A staff meeting? Professional interest group? Targeted intervention with staff from a specific year group?
- What information do you need to share with them?
- Do you want to modify or pilot this prior to sharing with all staff?
- How do you think learners and their families will respond?
- Are there any learners and families you could pilot this with?
- Do you need further information? (Remember you can ask questions via the Essential SENCO Forum for free at www.willowtreelearning.co.uk)

Reflections...

- Could this approach be useful to you at this time?
- Who else might be interested in reading about this?
- What do you need to do next?

7. The 7 Cs Progress Tracker

If you have just read Chapters 5 and 6, it is hoped that you are now feeling inspired and intrigued about the possible application of the 7 Cs Learning Portfolio in your school or setting. You may be feeling excited by the prospect of celebrating the strengths of all learners, as well as identifying the barriers to learning and their areas for development. It is hoped that the simplicity of the approach is also appealing and that you are beginning to see the potential for application. But hang on, how will you be able to capture progress?

As every SENCO and SEN Practitioner knows, it is essential that we can demonstrate 'anticipated' and 'actual' impact of our actions, even more so when these actions are 'additional to or different from the curriculum'. At a time of ever-increasing financial limitations and accountability, the need to demonstrate positive impact, outcomes and value for money regarding SEN provision has never been so great. **You may also feel pressure from a variety of internal and external sources to increase curriculum attainment, so how can you justify time and resources on interventions that are not directly curriculum related and how would you be able to show progress?**

Firstly the 7 Cs Learning Portfolio is a language of assessment that is directly curriculum related (after all curriculum is one of the Cs.) Furthermore, all of the other six Cs are skills that are necessary to ensure greater curriculum access. As outlined in Chapter 1, curriculum assessment for learners with SEND is a core entitlement so will be happening anyway. The 7 Cs Learning Portfolio is intended to offer a language of assessment to inform the action that is 'additional to or different from' the differentiated curriculum, which is intended to overcome or, where possible, remove barriers to learning. As such, there is a strong case for application. Capturing progress towards removing or overcoming barriers to learning is often cited by SENCOs as an area of concern and challenge. These are often referred to as 'soft' targets or 'anecdotal' or case study information. To promote confidence and to support the evidence-basing of progress within the 7 Cs Learning Portfolio, a Progress Tracker has been developed.

The 7 Cs Progress Tracker has been designed as a tool to capture starting points for each area and to scope possible development and improvement. It is qualitative in nature and is based on a collective judgement between the learner, parent/carer and teacher, of a 'best fit' score. The Progress Tracker uses a rating scale of 1–10, plotted within five phases of progress. The five phases of progress are outlined below:

Emerging – rating scale 1–3 (blue in colour)

Evolving – rating scale 4–6 (yellow in colour)

Effective – rating scale 7–9 (green – as it combines blue and yellow)

Enhanced – rating scale 10 (lime – an enhanced green)

Exceptional – rating scale 10+ (purple in colour)

It is important to stress that the effective phase or rating scale 7–9, should be the phase that is ultimately strived for. Of course, for many learners this may take significant time, and all progress should be valued, however small it appears within the rating scale. **The enhanced and exceptional phases should, by definition, be considered to have occasional relevance for some individual learners. It is not deemed appropriate to aim for the enhanced or exceptional phase, but rather it should be acknowledged if evidenced.** Of greater significance is the use of the rating scale, both to capture the starting point and to help capture impact and perceived progress. It is important to recognise that many of the skills and attributes within the 7 Cs Learning Portfolio are indeed lifelong skills; as such, progress may be minimal. **The value should not be placed upon the rating scale 'number' or progression of phase, but rather in the conversation about learning and the celebration of success and engagement with the learner themselves.** Although the Progress Tracker attempts to provide a language of 'evidence' of progress, it remains subjective and irrelevant without the conversation and direct engagement between the teacher, the learner and their parents or carers. It is essential that we value progress and achievement, but we must not confuse that with the value placed on the apparent statistical presentation of that progress. That said, the Progress Tracker is designed to help capture the diversity of learning and progress beyond the curriculum, which should be celebrated in all learners.

This Progress Tracker is a framework for capturing 'achievement' rather than 'attainment.' So often in education we interchange the words achievement and attainment, yet in fact here they are deemed to be different concepts. Achievement refers to a personal gain or development and to success towards a given aim. Attainment refers to acquired knowledge or specific skills relating to a common framework such as the curriculum. **Learners can be considered as being high-, mid- or low-attainers, with regards to curriculum skills and knowledge. But learners should not be described as low-achieving.** That learner may have achieved a great deal that day, simply by being at school, or perhaps from achieving success with a computer game or musical instrument. **We must remain mindful of the language that we use to describe children and young people and ensure that we do not simply generalise or assume that low curriculum attainment implies low achievement.**

The 7 Cs Progress Tracker has been designed for conversation, perhaps as part of an SEN Support planning or review meeting. A suggested starting point is to use the Progress Tracker to agree a 'baseline' for the three strengths and three areas for development that have been discussed between the teacher, learner and their family. For example, if it has been agreed that working memory is an area for targeted action, time would be spent agreeing the rating scale that best captures current skills. Similarly, as part of the review cycle, consideration may be given as to whether the 'best fit' rating scale has changed as a result of the targeted action. This can then be recorded as part of the assess, plan, do and review paperwork or using one of the 7 Cs Learning Portfolio recording sheets.

A further option is to use the Progress Tracker to record the baseline and to review progress recording the rating scale on the Progress Tracker record sheet. If your school or setting has access to Pupil Asset, you may wish to explore the use of the 7 Cs Learning Portfolio within this tool. This can be made available on request.

Cognition

Themes	Emerging 1–3	Evolving 4–6	Effective 7–9	Enhanced 10	Exceptional 10+
Working Memory	Small capacity so difficulties holding or retaining 1 or 2 pieces of information. Finds remembering instructions tricky and following requests.	Small to medium capacity. Able to hold 2–3 part instructions but loses 'details' tending to remember general elements or will fill in gaps.	Effective capacity so able to follow instructions and requests, holding reasonable amounts of information.	Larger capacity so able to hold and manipulate information beyond expectations.	Exceptional ability to hold, manipulate, reverse and sequence information.
Speed of Processing	Needs significant time to assimilate information or to complete tasks. Slow and requires scaffolding and prompting for each step.	Needs additional time to complete tasks or assimilate information, but is able to do so.	Effective assimilation of information and efficient use of time, so able to complete tasks within expected time.	Takes on information quickly and is highly efficient. Quick assimilation and application, so often completes tasks or provides answers before others.	Operating at exceptional speed and efficiency, assimilating information and completing tasks or requests.
Inference	Tendency to listen and repeat instructions, but not yet independently extracting implications. Interprets at a literal level and follows one step at a time.	Able to follow information and will answer questions posed, but without questions, may not infer for themselves.	Able to extract meaning and make predictions. Will stop, think and infer independently.	Able to infer meaning from information, contexts and apply experience to extract expectations.	Inference shows thoughtful reflection and independent extraction of implications. Evidence of higher order strategic thinking.

Cognition

Themes	Emerging 1–3	Evolving 4–6	Effective 7–9	Enhanced 10	Exceptional 10+
Anticipation	Highly impulsive and reactive, not yet able to 'anticipate' consequences or outcomes, instead blurts out.	Able to pause and consider with prompting and questioning. Responds to questions but not yet able to ask own questions to aid anticipation.	Able to pause, consider and identify different outcomes linked to an action.	Able to anticipate a series of actions or consequences, which could arise from more than one scenario.	Exceptional skill of anticipating actions, events and consequences, and is able to manoeuvre to promote desired outcome.
Reflection	Not yet able to think back or forwards to notice or consider actions or events. Operating within the present.	With prompting and scaffolding, actions are considered and noticed.	Independently able to notice and consider actions and consequences.	Actively notices and considers implications in order to identify potential modifications or differences to be used at another time.	Highly effective reflective thinking, seeking to notice actions and consequences.
Evaluation	Tendency to react to the 'immediate' choosing preferences based on recency rather than an informed weighing up.	Able to evaluate using a structured choice, choosing between two options given.	Independently able to weigh up real information or anticipated implications and make a proactive judgement.	Uses a range of sources and experiences in order to weigh up information. Actively triangulates and explores own reflections.	Confidently makes judgements based on triangulated information and sources, weighing up anticipated and actual outcomes.
Analysis	Responds to information literally and in isolation. Not yet able to consider against a criteria.	Able to focus on information when specifically presented or pointed out and consider it against criteria.	Effectively able to isolate and or combine a range of information against a specific criteria.	Highly effectively combines inference and evaluation and is able to analyse actual and anticipated information.	Uses analytical frameworks and systems to structure self directed review of information and potential outcomes.

Communication

Themes	Emerging 1–3	Evolving 4–6	Effective 7–9	Enhanced 10	Exceptional 10+
Expressive Vocabulary	Use of single words to name familiar objects.	Use of short phrases with a tendency to describe objects rather than naming. Some difficulties with recalling and grouping words.	Age-appropriate vocabulary which is applied fluently and accurately in communication. Able to identify categories and group words effectively.	Extensive vocabulary used accurately across a range of contexts. Enhanced understanding and categorisation of words.	Applied use of complex vocabulary exceeding age related expectations.
Articulation	Vocalisations are used to initiate and respond to communication. Some sounds and words are legible.	Many sounds and words are clear but specific sound patterns or words are not, which impact on the accuracy of speech.	Sounds and words are accurately and fluently pronounced and used effectively in speech.	Highly accurate and concise pronunciation of sounds and words, punctuated with a range of intonation and expression.	Exceptional accuracy and pronunciation possibly including more than one language.
Language & Comprehension	Emerging receptive vocabulary with an understanding of key or familiar words combined with a visual clue or object of reference.	Evolving knowledge of key words and application of contextual cues to aid understanding.	Age-appropriate comprehension and vocabulary enables understanding of spoken and written information.	Extensive understanding of language with a wide ranging receptive vocabulary. Effective application of inference and deduction when required.	Receptive language skills and vocabulary exceeding age expectations. Highly skilled inference and deduction to further aid comprehensive communication.
Collaborative Conversation	Tendency to blurt own views or repeat key phrases or requests, but not yet able to 'converse' adapting own speech in response to comments of others.	Use of turn taking within two or three part comments. Tendency to state own intended speech rather than make adaptations in response to comments of others.	Effectively engages within conversations, listening, turn taking, asking questions and responding and adapting own speech to comments of others.	Extensive range of questioning to explore comments of others. Able to develop comments that support or oppose other view to further expand conversation.	Exceptional insight and rigour applied to extend conversation, to provoke thought, reflection and analysis.

Communication

Themes	Emerging 1–3	Evolving 4–6	Effective 7–9	Enhanced 10	Exceptional 10+
Listening	Short attention with a tendency to 'hear' key words rather than listen to the whole. Preference for own agenda so may not share the 'need' to listen.	Some skills of active listening but tends to be time limited. Susceptible to distraction and may 'assume' understanding filling 'gaps' rather than listening in full.	Effectively applies active listening skills, demonstrating alertness and participation by extracting relevant information.	Highly attentive with extensive attention to detail. Focused and accurate in extracting information.	Exceptional attention and focus enables thoughtful and insightful active listening. Engagement that seeks clarification and extension of topic.
Social Communication (output)	Intermittent or non existent use of non verbal communication such as eye contact, gestures and personal space and or limited use of verbal language to initiate or respond to social communication.	Attempting to use verbal and non-verbal skills to initiate or respond to social communication with varying degrees of accuracy and appropriateness.	Effective use of verbal and non verbal skills to enable social communication. Good understanding of social contexts and cues, so able to initiate and respond to communication.	Confident and enhanced verbal and non-verbal communication skills so able to lead and promote communication from others.	Exceptionally able to promote empathy, connection and confidence from others, skillfully applying verbal and non verbal skills.
Social Interaction (input)	High levels of uncertainty and 'discomfort' associated with knowing 'how' to react to interaction from others. Regularly misunderstands comments, gestures or social expectations.	Attempting to apply 'learnt' rules or strategies to verbal and non-verbal interaction from others. Some accuracy, but lack of fluency or adaptability.	Effective social understanding and skills of inference, enables accurate responses to verbal and nonverbal interaction from others.	Insightful understanding of social interaction across all contexts. Responses are appropriate and adaptive.	Exceptionally insightful and confident in social situations. Able to accurately 'read' and anticipate verbal and non verbal interaction of others.

Creativity

Themes	Emerging 1–3	Evolving 4–6	Effective 7–9	Enhanced 10	Exceptional 10+
Generation of Ideas	Tends to work and think in the present, requires prompting and direction.	Attempts to repeat ideas of others with occasional expansion of idea.	Confident to generate and share original ideas and thoughts.	Generates creative ideas and builds upon thoughts and ideas of others.	Highly creative and original in thought, able to make connections and build ideas from self and others.
Problem-solving	Tendency to 'wait' for direction from others, not yet making connection between identifying the issue and contemplating actions to take.	Able to make 'random' suggestions which at times are highly appropriate and effective. Not yet strategic or consistent in approach.	Effective application of logic and creativity to find solutions, applying a systematic approach to problem solving.	Independent resolution of issues, applying efficient and logical strategy consistently to solve problems.	Exceptional skill of thinking logically and applying reasoning to define and resolve a problem in a wide and varied range of contexts.
Attention	Highly distractible with short attention. Not yet able to filter information with a tendency to 'flit' between stimuli.	Able to attend and focus for short periods of time, but during this time, additional stimuli is filtered and ignored.	Able to sustain attention, focus and filter distractions maximising concentration for an age appropriate amount of time.	High levels of attention and concentration for sustained periods of time regardless of context and distractions.	Ability to attend and focus within any context, screening out distractions to retain concentration even with less preferred tasks.
Motivation	Apathy and reluctance to engage in tasks or activities. Seeks to avoid or resist.	Eager and willing to complete tasks or activities of choice and self interest. Seeks to avoid or resist other tasks.	Age-appropriate interest, eagerness and willingness to complete a self directed or directed task or activity.	Active pursuit of tasks and activities promoting positivity and interest. Sustained 'desire' to complete activities to their conclusion.	Enthusiasm and interest to tasks and activities inspires others. Sustained authentic willingness and pursuit of enquiry.
Making Things	'Notices' materials and attempts to combine or explore, demonstrating some interest in tools or materials.	Growing interest in chosen materials and developing early skills required to engage with the 'build.' Increased accuracy and fluency with isolated skills.	Age-appropriate ability to construct, connect or make things using chosen materials. This could include Lego, junk modelling, craft, sewing, knitting, woodwork etc.	High levels of confidence, fluency and accuracy within chosen task or craft. Completed creations are admired.	Exceptional skill and accuracy within chosen area, resulting in consistent generation of reliable 'products' or 'builds.'

Creativity

Themes	Emerging 1–3	Evolving 4–6	Effective 7–9	Enhanced 10	Exceptional 10+
Courage & Determination	Tendency to 'give up' or assume inadequacy and seek support from others. Low self confidence, efficacy increases anxiety and reluctance to 'have a go.'	Attempts new or uncertain tasks and activities but requires assurance and encouragement. Not yet independent self belief.	Age-expected levels of courage and determination demonstrated across a range of contexts, resulting in sustained effort and visible 'have a go' attitude.	Highly courageous and tenaciously determined. Will apply new strategies and sustain efforts at times of adversity and challenge.	Inspires other with sustained courage and determination. Overcomes significant barriers and challenges and continues to retain motivation and enthusiasm.
Trust	High levels of insecurity and restricted confidence in others. Seeks to 'protect' self and avoid 'risk' or connections. Negative associations towards relationships with peers and or adults. Tend to isolate self.	Evolving levels of confidence and security with familiar adults and children. Will 'let guard' down within familiar contexts and is able to 'have a go' at tasks perceived to have limited risk.	Effective confidence in self and others so able to 'risk' and 'have a go.' Forms and sustains positive relationships with peers and adults and operates from a positive sense of security and belonging.	Confidence towards others and belief in self allows demonstration of 'vulnerability' and 'humanity.' Identifies the positives in all opportunities and sustains "belief' in self and others.	Exceptional belief in others inspires connection, attachments and positive interactions within all contexts. Unique ability to accept and value outcomes and to 'trust' self and others.

Control

Themes	Emerging 1–3	Evolving 4–6	Effective 7–9	Enhanced 10	Exceptional 10+
Self-regulation	Tendency to react to stimuli and lose regulation of behaviour, emotions and language. Can become over excited or angry and is not able to control, channel or redirect self at that time.	In some situations behaviour, feelings and language can be controlled for a short period of time. Attempts are made to channel or distract self, but not yet reliably consistent.	Age-appropriate control over behaviour, feelings and language. Able to calm, soothe, and regulate self most of the time.	Ability to 'notice' own signs of distress or arousal and mitigate to regulate behaviour, emotion or language, prior to any loss of control.	Exceptional consistency and self awareness of behaviour, emotions and language enabling control and self management.
Behaviour for Learning	Intentional or unintentional avoidance of learning tasks seeking to follow own agenda. May be distracted and or distracting, impacting on capacity to access learning at that time.	Increased willingness and readiness to engage and participate in activities of choice. Sustained distraction and reluctance in some areas.	Effective approach and attitude towards learning, demonstrating a readiness, willingness and the capacity to engage and participate.	Highly prepared and attempts to connect and anticipate learning opportunities for self. Consistently responsive to opportunities and actively seeks to apply for self.	Consistent enquiry combined with readiness and eagerness to engage in tasks. Seeks to develop learning of others as well as self, in order to maximise the context and opportunities for learning.
Anxiety Management	Anxious thoughts limit participation and engagement and negatively impact on well being and health. High levels of anxiety are experienced and are currently debilitating.	Anxious thoughts dominate and restrict engagement and participation and negatively impact on well being and health. Some strategies to aid the experience of anxiety are being rehearsed and at times implemented.	Anxiety is effectively identified and experienced. There is no loss of control due to fear or anxious thoughts, as these are 'noticed' and managed, most of the time.	Highly effective strategies are utilised at times of anxiety, so feelings are experienced but managed. Self awareness enables the use of protective strategies to mitigate anxiety where possible.	A range of strategies are available for use to support the experience of anxiety. Pre-emptive actions are taken to promote well being and resilience and to support the management of anxious thoughts.
Confidence	Tendency to seek support from others and reports a negative view of own capacity. High levels of insecurity and uncertainty result in a desire to avoid or distract from activities or goals.	Reluctant belief in self in some situations or contexts. Acknowledges some self capacity but not yet 'believe' in self.	Actions demonstrate a strong belief in self and own capacity to make a contribution, enabling a positive approach to challenge and attempting new activities.	Internal and external belief in own capacity combined with a humility to learn rather than an arrogance of knowing.	Exceptional confidence in self and own capacity promotes confidence from others. Assertive and resilient belief in self.

Control

Themes	Emerging 1–3	Evolving 4–6	Effective 7–9	Enhanced 10	Exceptional 10+
Resilience	High perception of 'failure' and inadequacy, resulting in a 'worn out' approach and reluctance to 'try again.' Deeply effected by knocks and simply unable at this time, to 'bounce' back.	Fragile approach to trying again. Likely to have one more go, but dependent on immediate 'success' or positive outcomes, to avoid sense of 'failure.'	Age appropriate tendency to 'bounce back' and to 'have another go.' Uses own sense of strengths and positive relationships to boost resiliency as and when depleted.	High levels of determination, focus and bounce back ability. Despite experiencing 'knocks' will continue to reflect and have another go. Inspiring others along the way.	Exceptionally effective strategies to protect self at times of challenge, exuberating the capacity to bounce back. Actively seeks to renew resiliency and maximise protective characteristics.
Language of Emotions	Not yet able to recognise or label emotions in self or others. Tends to present as 'overwhelmed' by emotions and not able to comprehend triggers of feelings.	Acquired a basic language of some emotions and can use picture cues or symbols to indicate feelings. Needs prompting to identify or share own feelings and to attempt to 'notice' in others.	Age-related language of emotions, so able to 'notice' feelings and to label them. Will talk to peers or adults about own feelings.	Highly developed language of emotions used to describe emotions noticed in self and others. Able to connect feelings to actions and to seek support if required.	Exceptionally intuitive and emotionally articulate when describing own feelings and 'noticing' feelings in others. High levels of empathy combined with shared language.
Independence	High need for support, assurance and direction. Not yet able to play or work alone, seeking instead adult or peer interaction and direction.	Able to play or work alone for short amounts of time during tasks or activities of own choosing. Continues to 'check in' with adults or peers and can become uncertain if left alone.	Age-appropriate self sufficiency, contentment and confidence promotes utilisation of own resources to achieve a task or activity. Able to work and play alone or with others.	Able to direct own focus and occupy self constructively engaging in tasks or activities alone. Uses initiative and presents as equally happy to adapt to working alone or with others.	Self sufficiency in relation to directing and managing behaviour, emotions and thoughts while also being able to share behaviour, emotions and thoughts with others as necessary. Exceptionally able to 'switch' from self sufficiency to collaboration as required.

Compassion

Themes	Emerging 1–3	Evolving 4–6	Effective 7–9	Enhanced 10	Exceptional 10+
Friendships	Ability to play alongside others or tolerate others playing near by. May use the word 'friend' but tends to generalise to any peer.	Able to identify a friend from other peers, and seeks to initiate and respond to interaction. Relationships can be fragile as may have a rigid or fixed expectation of the behaviour sought from peer. Not yet able to manage or resolve conflict.	Age-expected relationships with peers are formed and sustained over time. Able to manage low level conflict and disagreement, illustrating effective skills of compromise.	Identifiable friendships across a range of peers. Sustained and stable relationships over time. Able to connect with others and 'befriend' peers putting them at ease.	Consistently identified by others as a friend and has sustained relationships with peers over time. Connects with others across social contexts and demonstrates support and empathy with friends.
Turn-taking	Impulsive desire to blurt out and interrupt. Not yet able to 'wait' but seeks turn instantly. May have difficulties with sharing resources, people and space.	In some contexts, able to follow 'my turn, your turn' structure, but not yet able to wait for longer than one turn. Understands the concept and will attempt but control is limited.	Age-expected ability to wait and share resources, people and space. Management of internal desire to 'call out' or have a go, following turn taking 'rule.'	Able to wait for long periods of time and sustain focus and attention during other people's turns. Remains interested and motivated even when observing others.	Acceptance if another person interrupts, blurts out or takes turn. Remains patient and complies to embedded 'rule' of turn taking even if others do not.
Empathy	Tendency to only perceive from own perspective. Single view is rigid and absolute. Not yet able to consider impact on others, as only focus is impact on self.	Attempting to engage in activities that promote alternative perspectives and is able to acknowledge that variants may exist. Will listen to explanations of empathy and may be able to recite examples.	Age-expected ability to anticipate the experiences of others. Able to consider views from a perspective other than their own, attempting to understand.	Insightful anticipation of impact of experiences on others. Attempt to demonstrate this through compassion, understanding and care towards others.	Attempts to connect with others using insightful anticipation of the impact of other persons experiences and actively adjusting own behaviour for benefit of others.

Compassion

Themes	Emerging 1–3	Evolving 4–6	Effective 7–9	Enhanced 10	Exceptional 10+
Sense of Justice	Not yet aware of descriptors of 'right' and 'wrong' and tends to explore using cause and effect. Operates according to own view and perspective and seeks own goals.	Understands own sense of being 'wronged' or if someone does something 'right' but not yet consistent in analysis of own actions. Growing awareness from social stories and scenarios.	Effective sense of own ethical code and clear interpretation of 'right' and 'wrong.' Ability to advocate for perceived 'justice.'	Clarity regarding the rationale for own ethical code and an ability to describe this to others. Applies this within a range of contexts and is able to justify thinking.	Acknowledgement of different perspectives as motives for individual views regarding sense of justice. Displays a desire to reflect and understand differences and will explore alternative views and consider these within context of own views.
Self Esteem	Low sense of worth or value, unable to perceive strengths or contribution. In contrast, inflated sense of worth impacts on contribution as seen less important.	With support and prompting, able to identify strengths and times of worth and contribution. Greater acknowledgement of self and role offered.	Effective sense of value and worth, not excessively high or low, but generally has a positive sense of themselves.	Able to evidence base examples of 'worth' and 'value' which are used to enhance esteem and confidence.	Positive sense of worth and value provides a strong foundation for participation and engagement. Able to promote in others, as embedded within self.
Self-efficacy	Sense of indifference or ineffectual belief in own capacity. Why bother? May appear to switch off or become passive or helpless with limited or no engagement.	Starting to recall where change has happened if prompted by adult. Able to notice change in others and relate to own experiences. Responding to structured choices.	Age-expected belief in own capacity to effect change. They acknowledge that they make a difference and their voice counts.	Ability to identify 'evidence' of impact and change reinforcing sense of belief in own capacity to contribute.	Empowered belief in self and capacity to effect change. Underpins all actions and reactions, positively impacting on self and engagement.
Support for Others	Will let others be alongside and will share space and resources but tends to pursue own interest or agenda. Others can join them if they keep up.	Able to support others within a group context. Tends to follow the lead or actions of peers, will participate with anyone who joins the existing group.	Demonstrates kindness, support and compassion to peers and seeks to 'befriend' others. Viewed by adults as reliable and able to help others.	Seeks to promote interests of others before self. Will seek to help or connect with those who may be isolated or unhappy. Kind and considerate towards peers and adults.	Demonstrates empathy and 'notices' small details that help peers to feel valued. Consistent and reliable friend who shows compassion and acceptance to all.

Co-ordination

Themes	Emerging 1–3	Evolving 4–6	Effective 7–9	Enhanced 10	Exceptional 10+
Fine Motor Skills	Not yet able to accurately mark make or control equipment such as scissors or beads and may seek to avoid such tasks.	Developing accuracy of fine motor skill movements but not yet fluent with movements. Needs more time and concentration when completing tasks. (Tongue may protrude.)	Age-expected fluency and accuracy with fine motor movements so able to use scissors, write, draw, thread and manipulate small objects.	Highly efficient fine motor skills, demonstrating fluent and accurate control and dexterity of movements. Applies skills regularly within hobby or interests.	Exceptional accuracy of movements and control, able to complete small and delicate movements efficiently. Actively applies skills across a range of activities.
Gross Motor Skills	Lacks accuracy or fluency with control of isolated movements. Movements may appear broken rather than fluid.	Accuracy with movements but not yet fluent. Requires intense concentration and focus and can still lack fluidity.	Age-expected fluency and accuracy with gross motor movements. Able to run, jump, hop, throw, kick and catch a ball.	Highly skilled with gross motor movements, able to combine movements or complete in isolation.	Applies fluent and accurate gross motor skills within a range of activities and is deemed to be successful. Area of exceptional strength.
Sensory	Difficulties with hearing and or vision, may be diagnosed or under investigation. Impacts on communication and access to information.	Adjustments in place to 'overcome' the sensory barrier and gaining confidence and experience with adaptions.	Age-expected development of sensory skills. Good hearing and vision enables access to visual and auditory information.	Highly proficient hearing and or visual skills, perhaps with enhanced visual and or auditory processing skills.	Exceptional skill in one or more sensory area, used to enhance learning and deemed a considerable strength.
Mobility	Not yet independently mobile. May need support from adults or aids to facilitate movements.	Greater independence of movement either with or without aids. Limited fluency and ongoing need to further develop movements.	Age-expected mobility and or independent movement including walking, standing, running. Effective gait and step.	Significant fluency and agility of physical movements enables independent mobility and application of skills in to physically demanding activities.	Exceptional physical skill and mobility, enables application across sports and activities leading to personal success.
Stability & Balance	Requires supportive equipment or aids to provide stability and balance. Without it may lose control over.	Greater independent stability and balance but may occasionally 'wobble' or fall or trip over.	Age-expected stability and balance enables accurate movements and transitions in different contexts.	Highly stable and balanced so able to take part in physically active tasks and achieve success.	Exceptional stability and balance is utilised to pursue physical activities of interest. Deemed a significant strength.

Co-ordination

Themes	Emerging 1–3	Evolving 4–6	Effective 7–9	Enhanced 10	Exceptional 10+
Posture	Varies posture frequently, tends to fidget, wriggle and or slouch. Struggles to sustain effective writing posture.	Able to maintain effective posture for learning for short periods of time. Needs to change posture during and between tasks.	Age-expected posture when sitting and standing. Able to adapt posture to promote most effective access to learning.	Highly effective core muscles promotes appropriate posture across all contexts. Able to sustain attention and promote access to learning.	Exceptional core stability and posture used to promote access to learning and applied in to other activities such as dance, gymnastics, Pilates etc.
Sensory Processing	Huge discomfort or distress associated with hyper or hypo sensitivity to one or more sensory sources of information. Not yet able to process information and either seeks more or seeks to avoid.	Greater assimilation of some sensory sources in specific contexts. Able to screen out or filter individual sensory source at times.	Age-expected ability to assimilate sensory information. Able to filter, respond and extract sensory information from a range of contexts.	Highly tuned sensory information, able to filter and extract information across a number of sensory sources.	Exceptionally tuned sensory information so able to filter and extract information from any sensory source. Utilises sensory information to add to learning experience and recall.

Curriculum

Themes	Emerging 1–3	Evolving 4–6	Effective 7–9	Enhanced 10	Exceptional 10+
English	Significant barrier to learning linked to either or all: reading, writing, spelling and comprehension. Targeting development of phonics and sight words.	Developing greater accuracy with reading, writing, spelling and other age expected skills but lacks fluency and continues to require support or prompting.	Age-expected effective skills in reading, writing, spelling and comprehension. Able to access learning opportunities and actively participates in this subject.	Highly skilled and competent with reading, writing, spelling and comprehension. Independent application of skills across all subjects.	Exceptionally skilled and competent with reading, writing, spelling and comprehension. Utilises skills in pursuit of own interests and research.
Maths	Attempting to identify, order and sequence numbers and shapes. Not yet accurate with language of maths and needs adult prompting.	Developing greater accuracy with mathematical concepts and patterns, but lacks fluency and is not yet able to independently generalise rules. Seeks assurance and relies on prompts.	Age-expected understanding of number value, addition, subtraction, multiplication and division. Able to apply across contexts. Progressing within curriculum themes.	Fluent and accurate knowledge of number with skilful insight in to pattern, manipulation and sequencing. Good conceptual understanding and application of mathematical concepts.	Exceptionally skilled with number, shape, space and measure. Able to create and solve mathematical problems and connects methods. Deemed a significant strength.
Science	Able to look at objects and answer simple questions. Starting to identify and sort objects according to similarities and differences.	Curious about objects and the world around them and responds to guided questioning and exploration. Without the guidance, the approach may be 'random' rather than method based.	Age-expected levels of curiosity and intrigue about the world. Able to use a methodical structure to aid analysis. Will pose questions and seek answers.	Highly motivated to explore, understand and categorise information about themselves and the world. Connects information and able to hypothesise and test hypothesis.	Exceptional understanding and skills, epitomises a scientific approach. Seeks clarity, asks questions and challenges answers.
Art & Music	Some interest in sounds and instruments and or painting and modelling. Needs prompting to engage with activities and may only attempt for short amount of time.	Growing interest and experience with art and or music. Willing to explore and attempt activities, but lacks accuracy and fluency with tasks. Responds to praise, encouragement and questioning.	Age-expected skills in art and music. Keen to engage with a range of tasks and responds to questioning and reflection. Able to express preferences between genres.	Highly skilled within art and or music, demonstrating talent and personal accomplishments. Keen to exhibit or perform, sharing skills with others.	Exceptional talent or gift within art and or music. Significant accomplishments have boosted confidence and further enhanced skills.

Curriculum

Themes	Emerging 1–3	Evolving 4–6	Effective 7–9	Enhanced 10	Exceptional 10+
History & Geography	Working to understand concepts of time (past, present and future) and placement of events in to chronological sequence. Interest in exploring information presented but not yet independently.	Developing subject specific vocabulary and increasing conceptual knowledge with support from others. Participates in tasks but not consistently connecting the information or learning.	Age-expected skills in history and geography. Accessing curriculum opportunities and attempting to make connections between topics.	Significant skill and interest in subjects and is fluent and accurate with subject vocabulary and concepts. Extends own learning by pursuing additional information or enquiries.	Exceptional skill and fluency with subject matter. Applies information effectively and generates additional learning for self and others through research and questioning.
Computing	Able to explore visual information using a touchscreen tablet. Follows direction and will attempt tasks, but not yet applying independently.	Greater fluency and accuracy within ICT of choice, (e.g. gaming or use of tablets.) Needs prompting with programming and some reluctance to engage with directed tasks.	Effective skills with computing and displays age related knowledge of technology. Able to use some tools independently to aid learning.	High levels of fluency and confidence within subject. Utilises equipment to aid independent learning and to pursue social interests and communication.	Exceptional skill of programming and utilising ICT to achieve outcomes. Able to support access of others and pursue own interests.
PE & Sport	Attempt to engage with activities but lacks fluency and accuracy with movements. May struggle with pace of activities and movements.	Developing greater skill accuracy and interest in PE and Sports but lacks fluency and may not keep pace with peers in all contexts.	Effective skills and competency within PE and Sports. Participates in a range of activities and is able to assimilate rules for each. Good sense of own health and fitness.	Significant skill and interest in PE and Sports. Participates with others in team sports and connects nutrition, fitness and health and well being.	Exceptional skill across PE and Sport. Participates within sports at competitive level and is deemed to be successful. Good understanding of impact on health and well being.

The 7 Cs Learning Portfolio
Action Assessment Record

Pupil Name: Harry Cooper   **Date of Birth: 8-12-14**   **Year Group: 3**   **Completed by: JC Class Teacher**

Autumn Term:

Area of Learning	Element of Learning	Date & Rating Scale	Progress	Date & Rating Scale	Progress
Cognition	Working Memory	15–9–19 Emerging 3	1–11–19 Emerging 3	Maintained	18-12-19 Evolving 4	+1
Communication	Listening	15–9–19 Evolving 5	1–11–19 Evolving 6	+ 1	18-12-19 Effective 7	+1
Control	Resilience	15–9–19 Evolving 4	1–11–19 Evolving 5	+1	18-12-19 Evolving 6	+1

Spring Term:

Area of Learning	Element of Learning	Date & Rating Scale	Progress	Date & Rating Scale	Progress
Control	Resilience	12–1–20 Evolving 6	22-2-20 Effective 7	+1	4-4-20 Effective 7	maintained
Control	Confidence	12–1–20 Evolving 5	22-2-20 Effective 7	+2	4-4-20 Effective 7	maintained
Compassion	Friendships	12–1–20 Evolving 4	22-2-20 Evolving 6	+2	4-4-20 Effective 7	+1

Summer Term:

Area of Learning	Element of Learning	Date & Rating Scale	Progress	Date & Rating Scale	Progress
Cognition	Working Memory	25-4-20 Evolving 4	28-5-20 Evolving 4	maintained	5–7–20 Evolving 5	+1
Creativity	Problem Solving	25-4-20 Emerging 3	28-5-20 Evolving 4	+1	5–7–20 Evolving 6	+2
Compassion	Self-Efficacy	25-4-20 Emerging 3	28-5-20 Evolving 4	+1	5–7–20 Evolving 6	+2

The 7 Cs Learning Portfolio Action Assessment Record

Pupil Name:

Date of Birth:

Year Group:

Completed by:

Autumn Term:

Area of Learning	Element of Learning	Date & Rating Scale	Progress	Date & Rating Scale	Progress

Spring Term:

Area of Learning	Element of Learning	Date & Rating Scale	Progress	Date & Rating Scale	Progress

Summer Term:

Area of Learning	Element of Learning	Date & Rating Scale	Progress	Date & Rating Scale	Progress

Implications for SENCOs and SEN Practitioners

The 7 Cs Learning Portfolio and Progress Tracker provide a complete framework that can facilitate a shared language of assessment and a tool for capturing progress. It may be useful to consider a learner that you know well or whose SEN Support meeting is due soon and see if they can help you start to apply the tools for yourself.

The 7 Cs Learning Portfolio provides a language of assessment that enables the identification of strengths and barriers to learning – the purpose being to celebrate the skills and talents of every learner and to consider how these can be utilised and built upon to overcome and/or remove barriers to learning. For example, if we know that a learner has good friendship skills, we may use friends as peer supporters to help the development of phonological awareness skills, if this is a current barrier to learning. It also ensures that we promote the strengths and 'notice' the skills of the learner and do not just focus on their needs for improvement. The Progress Tracker offers a framework for conversation and helps to capture progress relative to starting point.

Reflections...

- Could the Progress Tracker help to capture the 'starting point' or baseline for a learner?
- How accessible would this be for staff?
- What would be the most effective way of sharing this with staff?

8. Collaborating with learners and families

Effective assessment should directly include the learner and those that know them the best. Families obviously know their children and young people the best although staff working with children and young people have an essential insight into the learner's experience of learning. The learner is, however, the 'expert' of themselves, thus utilising this expertise is crucial. So often, assessment is something that is done 'to' a learner but is most effective when it is done 'with' them. Once again, the key to achieving this, is to develop a shared language of assessment. Black and William (1998) discussed the need to 'train' pupils in self-assessment. The 7 Cs Learning Portfolio User Guide has been written to enable a sharing of language around assessment. This is not the same as training in self-assessment, but a shared language is arguably a first step. The second step links to experience of making judgements.

Enabling learners to make judgements about their learning is at the heart of this model. Of course, it may be that the child or young person has an inflated judgement of their skills or indeed difficulties. Similarly, they may underestimate their skills and difficulties. The use of a rating scale can help to 'balance' that judgement, as numerical descriptors can be given. It may also be relevant to record the teacher scale, the pupil scale and the parent/carer scale; after all, if these are significantly different, this could in itself be useful information. The important point is to facilitate the experience of making a self-evaluation and judgement about learning, using a shared language.

It is for this reason that a letter template from a teacher to a learner has been developed. The aim is to share this with children, young people and their families to encourage active participation in the learning conversation, identifying their three strengths and three areas for development.

Example 7 Cs Learning Portfolio – Learner Letter

Dear Jake

You are invited to a learning review meeting with a member(s) of your Family which will take place at school on 18-3-21 at 3.30pm. At the meeting we will talk about how you are getting on at school and at home and we will think about 3 things that you are really good at, which we will call your strengths. We will also talk about 3 things that you are finding more difficult, which are your areas for development. We will give each of your strengths a number from 1 to 10 where 10 is the highest mark and do the same for the 3 areas we have identified for development. These numbers will help us remember your 'starting point' so when we meet again, we will be able to see if there are any changes. Change can take time, so don't worry too much about the numbers, what is important is what we talk about and what we decide to do to help you develop in these areas. To help me, I will use the 7 Cs Learning Portfolio which is a little booklet which describes lots of learning skills. They are grouped into 7 words beginning with C, these are:

Cognition – these are our thinking skills

Communication – these are our skills for talking, listening and understanding

Creativity – this is how we think and whether we can build, make or bake things

Control – this is about how we manage our feelings, words and actions.

Compassion – this is the skills we use to show our feelings to others

Co-ordination – this is how we control and organise how our body moves

Curriculum – these are our skills with subjects and topics taught at school

It would be really useful if you and your family could start to think about what you think you are good at and what you find a bit more difficult. You can then share these ideas at our meeting.

Many thanks

Ms Carter

This letter may also be useful to share with parents/carers, along with the 7 Cs Learning Portfolio User Guide and/or A4 booklet. Of course, in the same way that every child is an individual, so is every parent or carer. As such, you may want to adjust the presentation of this information to suit the child and family. For example, if you prefer verbal communication with families, share this information in person. If you send text messages or make phone calls, adapt the information accordingly. The purpose is to develop a shared language of assessment and to empower the learner and their family to actively participate and contribute to this process.

7 Cs Learning Portfolio – Learner Letter

Dear,

You are invited to a learning review meeting with a member(s) of your Family which will take place at school on .... at .... At the meeting we will talk about how you are getting on at school and at home and we will think about 3 things that you are really good at, which we will call your strengths. We will also talk about 3 things that you are finding more difficult, which are your areas for development. We will give each of your strengths a number from 1 to 10 where 10 is the highest mark and do the same for the 3 areas we have identified for development. These numbers will help us remember your 'starting point' so when we meet again, we will be able to see if there are any changes. Change can take time, so don't worry too much about the numbers, what is important is what we talk about and what we decide to do to help you develop in these areas. To help me, I will use the 7 Cs Learning Portfolio which is a little booklet which describes lots of learning skills. They are grouped in to 7 words beginning with C, these are:

Cognition – these are our thinking skills

Communication – these are our skills for talking, listening and understanding

Creativity – this is how we think and whether we can build, make or bake things.

Control – this is about how we manage our feelings, words and actions.

Compassion – this is the skills we use to show our feelings to others.

Co-ordination – this is how we control and organise how our body moves.

Curriculum – these are our skills with subjects and topics taught at school.

It would be really useful if you and your family could start to think about what you think you are good at and what you find a bit more difficult. You can then share these ideas at our meeting.

Many thanks

Example 7 Cs Learning Portfolio – Parent/Carer Letter

Dear Mr Brown

Jake has been given a letter inviting him and a member(s) of his family to attend a learning review meeting at school on 18-3-21 at 3.30pm. The purpose of the meeting is to talk about how he is getting on at school and at home and, to identify 3 strengths and 3 areas for development. These areas for development will become the focus of the SEN Support provided to Jake during the next half term.

In school we use the 7 Cs Learning Portfolio, which helps us to talk to children about all aspects of learning, not just the curriculum. Of course, the curriculum is one of the Cs, but the other Cs include Cognition, Communication, Creativity, Control, Compassion and Co-ordination. I attach the A4 booklet/User Guide for your information. If time allows, please could you start to think of Jake's strengths and any areas for development that you see, or he talks to you about? We will be able to share our ideas at this meeting and then try to plan if Jake can use his strengths to help his future learning.

I look forward to seeing you at the meeting. If you have any questions, please do not hesitate to contact me.

Best wishes

Judith Carter

7 Cs Learning Portfolio – Parent/Carer Letter

Dear,

.... has been given a letter inviting him and a member(s) of his family to attend a learning review meeting at school on .... at .... The purpose of the meeting is to talk about how he is getting on at school and at home and, to identify 3 strengths and 3 areas for development. These areas for development will become the focus of the SEN Support provided to .... during the next half term.

In school we use the 7 Cs Learning Portfolio which helps us to talk to children about all aspects of learning, not just the curriculum. Of course, the curriculum is one of the Cs, but the other Cs include Cognition, Communication, Creativity, Control, Compassion and Co-ordination. I attach the A4 booklet/User Guide for your information. If time allows, please could you start to think of ....'s strengths and any areas for development that you see, or he talks to you about? We will be able to share our ideas at this meeting and then try to plan if .... can use his strengths to help his future learning.

I look forward to seeing you at the meeting. If you have any questions, please do not hesitate to contact me.

Best wishes

....

Implications for SENCOs and SEN Practitioners

It is essential that staff are confident with a language of assessment, in this case, with the language of the 7 Cs Learning Portfolio. This will empower them to converse with parent/carers and learners about learning and not just the curriculum. Once this is achieved, they, with you, may begin to consider how to create a shared language for assessment that is accessible to learners and their families. It may be that you decide to use a parent/carer SEN forum to introduce the 7 Cs Learning Portfolio to families. You may also choose to host a pupil focus group to introduce the language too. Or as a whole school you may plan an annual 'Learning Festival' which includes talks and activities that rehearse skills from each of the 7 Cs. You may also integrate the 7 Cs Learning Portfolio into your SEN information report, if this becomes part of your process of identifying educational needs. The greater the consistency of application of this language, the greater the potential impact.

Reflections...

- Are there any learners who may immediately benefit from using the 7 Cs Learning Portfolio?
- What existing opportunities could be utilised to share this approach with staff and families?
- How do we currently celebrate learning with our families across our school or setting?

References

Inside the Black Box: Raising Standards through Classroom Assessment (1998) Paul Black and Dylan William. Brentford, London: GL Assessment.

9. Intervention

As you have now reached the penultimate chapter in this book, it is hoped that you are feeling enthused, motivated and are having lots of creative thoughts about your next steps regarding the 7 Cs Learning Portfolio. Perhaps you are nearing a decision about application. Functional, intermediate or extensive? You may have identified the staff (in your head) who you think you will discuss this with first. You may even have chosen the date for the staff meeting, where you will be able to present this to colleagues. But hang on, what if you do adopt this approach to assessment and you do identify three strengths and three areas for development for your learners at SEN Support, what next? How do you overcome or remove these barriers to learning?

As we discovered in Chapter 1, the ultimate purpose of assessment is to inform 'action'. With regards to SEN assessment, it is about identifying action that is 'additional to or different from' the differentiated curriculum – **remembering, of course, that every child has an entitlement to a differentiated curriculum, so anything 'extra' is extra; it builds on this entitlement, it does not replace it.** Teachers will still differentiate maths tasks, but the learner may also have an opportunity to rehearse memory or language skills too. So OK, your staff, parents/carers and pupils now all have a shared language of assessment, but do they have a language of or tools to support intervention?

The intervention itself should be informed by what might overcome or remove the barrier to learning or improve the area for development. Interventions that seek to overcome the barrier to learning can be 'tweaks' or adjustments to improve quality-first teaching. Or it might involve the introduction of an additional adult or peer supporter who attempts to mediate or facilitate access to the learning task. Intervention that seeks to remove the barrier to learning may include targeted teaching of a skill or opportunities to rehearse and develop greater efficiency with a skill, so it no longer is an area for development. Alas, it is not possible to generate a 'definitive' list of interventions for every barrier to learning, as the experience of a barrier to learning is individual to that learner, so our responses should be individual to that learner too. However, to support your thinking and to offer a starting point regarding actions to overcome or remove barriers to learning identified within the 7 Cs Learning Portfolio, the following ideas are presented.

7 Cs Cognition – Learning Element	Action to 'Overcome' Barrier	Action to 'Remove' Barrier (where possible)
Working Memory	• Ensure concise & simple instructions • Encourage and teach paraphrasing • Teach note taking and use of mind maps • Reduce memory overload providing prompts and recapping • Take photos of information on the board or use voice recording or instructions for playback • Explicit teaching of how to use technology to aid recall, e.g. camera, voice recorder, lists, alarms on a phone or tablet. • Teacher to voice record instructions on to tablet for pupil to replay.	• Up until the age of 14 years old, play memory games intended to develop skill and efficiency of recalling: Pairs, Snap, 'I went shopping' • Rehearse activities such as those in the *Working Memory Activities: A Workbook to Stimulate Memory Skills* by David Newman, 2014
Speed of Processing	• Ensure sufficient time given for tasks (request additional time in exams) • Use visual prompts, recapping and paraphrasing • Work with peer buddies • Actively 'chunk' and 'scaffold' information	• Rehearse reaction time tasks such as Snap, Hungry Hippos, Buckaroo, etc. • Play comprehension games and activities applying time limits and seeking to 'beat' own scores.
Inference	• Use questions to structure use of information. • Model examples of 'inference' and explicitly define the process • Highlight key text and link to a specific question.	• Discuss short texts or stories, explicitly modelling how to identify key information and infer meaning from it. • Rehearse social scenarios and consider interpretation and perspective. • Role play conversations and discussions
Anticipation	• Use structured choices to offer 'possible' action that could be anticipated. • Work within a small group and explicitly model the anticipation process.	• Provide structured opportunities for 'what if' games, where topics or scenarios are discussed and predictions made. • Watch films or listen to stories and 'pause' at relevant points to encourage discussion and prediction.

Reflection	• Refer back to prior experiences or activities and model examples of reflection. • Ask "so what did we learn?" type questions to the class or small group, providing structured prompts as necessary.	• Small group time explicitly teaching reflective practice using structured questions such as what happened? What was good about that? Would I do it differently? • Use of social scenarios to provoke reflective thought and discussion.
Evaluation	• Ask "how do you know this?" type questions encouraging the class or small group to listen to information and to weigh up advantages and disadvantages. • Create a culture of 'decision-making' where class members choose between structured choices about recording materials (writing or typing), sitting at table or on floor, working alone or in pairs.	• Explicitly teach process of weighing up information, through small group discussion and verbal illustration of process. • Use structured questions to 'scaffold' evaluative process and rehearse application in pairs or small groups.
Analysis	• Ask "why do you think this?" type questions encouraging individuals to analyse own actions or thoughts about an activity or information from a lesson. • Provide opportunities for learners to focus on details and to explore implications of details.	• Use structured questions to 'scaffold' analysis process including eliciting details and considering similarity, differences, relevance and other implications. • Explicitly teach how to focus on the macro and micro and provide opportunities for considering both. Enable learners to work in pairs or small groups to rehearse the skill.

7 Cs Communication – Learning Element	Action to 'Overcome' Barrier	Action to 'Remove' Barrier (where possible)
Speech – Expressive Vocabulary	• Use pictures or symbols to promote non-verbal communication. • Teach 'priority' vocabulary as single words to aid communication. • Use "I wonder" phrases to reflect possible feelings or thoughts that the child may be having and to model speech. • Provide sufficient time to allow the Learner to attempt communication.	• Explicitly teach vocabulary starting with key and priority words to aid communication. • Explicitly teach category words and prepositions. • Play 'word' games that identify objects and sequencing. • Seek additional information from a Speech and Language Therapist and implement an individualised programme.
Speech – Articulation	• Provide sufficient time to allow the Learner to attempt to use speech and or combine with visual prompts or symbols. • Work with friend to promote security and to aid joint communication.	• Explicitly rehearse the articulation of sounds and words playing word or letter games. • Provide opportunities for singing and sound making. • Seek additional information from a Speech and Language Therapist and implement an individualised programme.
Language	• Ensure use of simple instructions and where possible combine with a visual prompt or 'modelled' example. • Encourage paired or small group working with supportive peers.	• Explicitly teach meanings of words and increase receptive vocabulary playing word games, sharing stories and pictures. • Teach category words to help structure recall and meaning. • Teach the learner to use devices such as 'Alexa' or 'Siri' to ask for the meaning of words. • Seek additional information from a Speech and Language Therapist and implement an individualised programme.

Collaborative Conversation	• Play structured games which require turn taking, guided by an adult. • Use role play to explicitly model and teach collaborative listening. For example, facilitate 'phone conversations' or 'interview' scenarios where questions are asked and answered in turn.	• Adults may be required to 'structure' or 'broker' conversations between the Learner and peers, modelling 'my turn, your turn.' • Intervene to reduce emerging conflict and seek to model or summarise conversation points.
Listening	• Provide opportunities for extended focus and explicit extraction of key information, such as playing 'treasure hunt' activities where key information is verbally given. • Play games that involve a specific 'action' when the learner 'hears' a specific word. For example, putting their hand up when they hear a key word in a story, or standing up for another word. • Use reading comprehension tasks verbally to teach the identification of key words in sentences.	• Ensure verbal information is concise and combined with a visual prompt. • Scaffold tasks to include prompts and guides. • If the Learner is an effective reader, provide written instructions to accompany verbal information. • Use the Learner's name at the start of an instruction and ask the Learner to paraphrase information.
Social Communication (output)	• Explicitly teach and rehearse key phrases to use as sentence starters or social 'ice breakers.' • Explicitly teach and rehearse the use of non-verbal communication signals • Rehearse social scenarios and identify effective and non-effective communication skills.	• Broker communication between the learner and peers – an adult may seek to 'interpret' or give additional information to the peer to enable greater understanding. • Facilitate shared activities and joint interests to 'prompt' discussion and informal communication.
Social Interaction (input)	• Explicitly teach and rehearse social situations and 'possible' responses or reactions. Link each reaction to an action that the learner can then safely apply. • Explicitly teach safe 'closing' responses, such as "OK then" or "If that's what you think." • Explicitly teach and rehearse skills of concern or sources of anxiety, using social stories to aid future application.	• Broker interaction between the learner and peers – an adult may need to intervene to 'explain' a response or a reaction. • Seek to 'avoid' conflict or anxiety by stepping in and redirecting or seeking to 'label' and explain interaction. • Provide 'safe space' or time out area where learner can safely retreat to.

7 Cs Creativity – Learning Element	Action to 'Overcome' Barrier	Action to 'Remove' Barrier (where possible)
Generation of Ideas	• Provide suggestions or options and encourage learners to explore feasibility of the idea and express a preference. • Provide opportunities for the Learner to work with other peers who may 'model' idea generation. • Change the 'modality' of expression – encouraging the learner to draw their idea or to build it from blocks as an alternative to verbally saying it.	• Establish opportunities for the Learner to explore 'what happened next' scenarios where there are no right or wrong answers but children think of possibilities. • Encourage the learner to build, create, draw, make or bake developing their own ideas for action. • Ensure all learners have an opportunity to 'be in charge' and suggest actions for others.
Problem-solving	• Provide structured choices and ask the learner to identify one of three ideas. • Use questions to encourage them to reflect on what information they have and what information they need? • Provide opportunities to work in pairs or small groups to observe the actions of peers.	• Explore scenarios and explicitly teach how to identify options and to consider the consequences of each action. • Provide resources or situations that require 'solving' such as how to transport a pencil from one desk to another without touching it. Explicitly model options for solving. • Use games and treasure hunt type puzzles to provide opportunities for problem solving.
Attention	• Use learner's name at the start of an instruction. • Ensure information is concise and ask the learner to paraphrase information. • Attempt to minimise or screen out distractions – consider working station or headphones.	• Explicitly teach 'focus' and attention skills using approaches such as 'attention autism.' • Ask the learner to attempt different screening devices (headphones, work station, listening to music) and to try different postures – standing, sitting, kneeling, laying and ask them to select the one that helps them focus for longer.
Motivation	• Praise and encourage • Use positive rewards system • Link to a now and next structure • Share success with people the learner nominates: friends in another class or send a text to their family member.	• Work with the learner to identify the 'rationale' for a task, skill or activity and ask them to identify how this could help them? • Encourage the learner to set own goals and to anticipate what success will feel like and who they will share their success with. • Use coaching approaches to promote ownership and self-direction of goals and achievements.

Making Things	• Explicitly teach techniques and skills of cutting, measuring and connecting materials. • Explicitly teach how to follow instructions or recipes and provide opportunities for rehearsal. • Scaffold learning by breaking the task in to small steps and providing feedback after each step.	• Provide many and varied opportunities to make things using a range of stimuli. • Work in a pair or small group to create a collaborative project. • Model techniques and skills or watch others on YouTube prior to having a go.
Courage – Determination	• Use coaching techniques to identify goals and aspirations. Work with the learner to identify actions that could be taken to achieve the goals and identify difficulties and risks. • Explicitly describe feelings of courage and bravery to 'have a go' at something new or difficult. • Provide opportunities for learners to attempt new and unfamiliar tasks. Explicitly label their desire to attempt this as courage. • Use stories and social scenarios that illustrate courage and determination and discuss the feelings associated with this.	• Promote a culture of 'having a go' and build in an expectation of mistakes. Introduce the concept of '5 lives' (using the fingers on their hand) so they can have a go and if they are wrong, have another go. • Praise and model 'sustained effort.' Vocalise thoughts of uncertainty when approaching a new task, but demonstrate actions and efforts. • Label actions that show courage and determination and praise the learner in those moments.
Trust	• Explicitly talk about trust and how it feels to trust and not to trust. Describe the feelings and actions within a small focus group. Ask the learner to identify when they would trust someone and when they would not. • Use social stories and social scenarios to illustrate examples to trust.	• Remain consistent, fair and predictable in interactions with the learner. • Model times of trust, labelling the feelings and explaining why it is ok to trust in that situation. For example, trusting the learner to deliver an errand and reinforcing that they have all of the skills required to do this.

7 Cs Control – Learning Element	Action to 'Overcome' barrier	Action to 'Remove' Barrier (where possible)
Self-regulation	• Access to a 'safe' place to calm down such as a "think tent" or "contemplation corner" where learner can retreat to. • Positive adult intervention using questions and reminders of 'signs' of distress or anxiety. • Positive re-direction to 'break' negative cycle of emotions – sending learner on an errand, adopting a sensory break or mindful colouring or building.	• When the learner is calm and regulated discuss the angry feelings and signals that they can 'notice' and explicitly link to an action that can be taken. Rehearse the application of this. • Explicitly teach mindfulness, yoga or Pilates techniques to help focus breathing and to promote ownership of calming strategies. • Proactively plan reflection and conversation time where the learner is encouraged to discuss feelings using rating scales or emoticons to aid description.
Behaviour for Learning	• Provide simple verbal and visual reminders of behaviours required for learning – looking, listening etc. • Ensure that information is concise and accessible, check out the learner's understanding by asking them to paraphrase what they need to do. • Positive rewarding and praising for learning behaviours, explicitly linking the behaviour to learning.	• Explicitly teach listening and attention skills. • Explicitly teach note taking and or mind mapping to aid recall of instructions. • Explicitly teach and use a resources checklist with the learner, so they are prepared and organised for the task ahead.
Anxiety Management	• At times of anxiety reassure the learner that they are safe and ask them to identify what might help them. (Try to avoid telling them what might help them or seemingly 'fixing' the issue for them.) • Encourage the learner to remember what helps them when they feel worried – going to their 'quiet' space, reading a book, listening to music or colouring? • Where possible seek to pre-prepare the learner and give advance warning of change to events.	• At times of calm, encourage the learner to talk about their feelings and worries, identifying triggers. Work together to identify actions that could be taken by the learner when these feelings arise. Rehearse the application of these actions. • Listen to the learner and talk about the 'likelihood' of this happening. Use cognitive behavioural therapy approaches to encourage reflection on feelings and the impact on behaviours. • Rehearse 'comforting' strategies, such as holding their own hand, finger tracing, counting to 10, singing a favourite song and discuss how to apply these when anxiety strikes.

Category		
Confidence	• Use questions to encourage learner to identify their strengths and to apply these to the learning task. E.g., 'turn to the person next to you and share what skills do you already have that could help you with this task? • Model phrases and label feelings that are associated with feeling confident including "I can" statements.	• Individually or in small groups work with learners to identify times when they felt confident and explore what helped them to feel this. • Use stories to illustrate what confidence 'looks like' and ask the learner to keep a 'confidence log' or diary, where they capture times that they feel confident.
Resilience	• Create a class culture of 'try and try again'. Build a shared expectation that getting something 'wrong' is just the next step in getting it right at some point. • Adults model resilience by sharing uncertainty and (un)intentional errors and persevering despite this.	• Explicitly teach resilience skills within a small group. Using books such as *Bouncing Back and Coping with Change* by Tina Rae, 2016, which identify weekly activities for small groups. • Audit resiliency protective characteristics (such as literacy skills, friendships, humour,) and target opportunities for further developments. For example, ensure that the learner experiences success during every day and has an opportunity to 'laugh' with peers, breaking the negative cycle of perceived challenge and failure.
Language of Emotions	• Adults model a language of emotions and integrate these into lessons and conversations with learners. • Use emoticons or other visual images to illustrate feelings and encourage the class to select pictures that capture their feelings at intervals during the day. • Ask the class to relate feelings to a rating scale and 'check in' with learners asking how they feel at different times in the day.	• Explicitly teach and rehearse the naming of emotions working individually or in small groups. • Take photos of the learner when they exhibit different feelings and talk about how they look and feel at different points. Encourage the identification of physical changes in facial expressions to help identify feelings in themselves and others. • Use stories to illustrate feelings and to build an expectation that feelings constantly change. 'Normalise' the experience of all feelings and promote their identification.
Independence	• Provide opportunities for all learners to complete activities on their own such as completing a jigsaw puzzle, listening to an audio book, using an electronic tablet or pc. • Encourage adults to use questions to learners rather than provide answers. 'what should you be doing? What equipment will you need? Have you seen this before? What might help you? • Ensure that tasks are differentiated and accessible to the learner.	• Explicitly teach learning routines and provide visual prompt sheets including an equipment checklist. Rehearse 'getting started' on an activity. • Explicitly teach 'how I can help me' strategies, including question prompts and responses. Rehearse individually or in small groups. • Facilitate the completion of short and accessible tasks and praise independent completion. Cite this as evidence of ability and ensure the learner 'notices' their success.

7 Cs Compassion – Learning Element	'	Action to 'Remove' Barrier (where possible)
Friendships	• Broker friendships by identifying a 'peer pyramid' to play alongside the learner. • Introduce structured games at unstructured times to enable active participation and engagement. • Create a friendship bench or play area where children can play alongside each other. For older students seek to facilitate shared clubs or interest groups brokering interaction at unstructured times.	• Explicitly teach skills used to 'initiate' interaction and rehearse questions that can be asked to peers that promote positive engagement. • Establish a circle of friends with the learner who can 'look out' for them at unstructured times and seek to 'teach' effective skills.
Turn-taking	• Adult to model and broker turn-taking during short task with peer such as snap or pairs. • Ensure learner is working with a group of peers who will 'tolerate' impulsive actions and non-turn-taking. • Provide opportunities for learner to engage in tasks alone but alongside others.	• Explicitly teach turn-taking through play-based tasks with the adult. • Role play turn-taking playing language games or physical activities such as jumping, throwing beanbags etc.
Empathy	• Label 'possible' feelings of others while sharing stories or giving class examples and signpost the importance of thinking about how someone else might feel. • Adult may need to broker relationships and explain or 'interpret' feelings to learner or peer.	• Explicitly teach a language of feelings and use stories or social scenarios to encourage the learner to 'predict' how another person may feel. • Role play responses that show awareness of others, such as 'are you ok?' 'did that upset you?' 'I'm sorry you feel sad.'
Sense of Justice	• Create a consistent and 'fair' classroom culture and refer to shared expectations. Label 'gaps' in expectations and model consequences or implications. • Adult may need to broker relationships and friendships and intervene to manage conflict or frustration.	• Explicitly teach tools for managing conflict and frustration such as 'restorative' approaches. • Rehearse the application of tools using social scenarios or stories. • Explicitly teach how to 'use' time out and model stages of thinking and feeling.

Self-esteem & Wellbeing	• Use positive language to 'reflect' comments back to the learner signposting their positive attributes or achievements. • Create a 'compliments' culture in the class, where peers give compliments to each other identifying their success and achievements. • Use positive rewards and praise to highlight skills and achievements.	• Ask the learner to identify what they have been successful at each day. (They may need to be given 2 or 3 examples but they should then choose 1 of these.) • Individually or in small groups, identify strengths and feelings. Recall times of feeling happy, successful, helpful etc. • Create a 'celebration' journal where the learner is able to record times of success and achievement.
Self-efficacy	• Build in opportunities for the learner to make choices and to effect change, such as choosing whether to use pen or pencil, choosing which group to work with. • Use structured choices to help scaffold decision making. • If the learner has been absent from school, welcome them back adding that their ideas were 'missed.'	• Individually or in small groups explicitly rehearse social situations or scenarios where the learner is able to 'impact' or influence change. Label this and evidence base the impact to the learner. • Provide regular opportunities to meet with the Learner to identify times of impact and success. Use coaching techniques to support the identification and achievement of goals (using resources within *Life Coaching for Kids* by Nikki Giant.)
Support for Others	• Provide opportunities for the learner to work and play alongside peers who are supportive and tolerant of impulsive responses. • Encourage learner to identify a positive action taken by someone else and to thank or praise them. • Teach team or paired games and broker relationships to enable shared play.	• Use stories and social scenarios to explicitly model examples of 'supporting others.' Discuss the feelings associated with these actions. • Role play using 'scripts' or 'conversation starters' to initiate play and interaction with others.

7 Cs Co-ordination – Learning Element	Action to 'Overcome' Barrier	Action to 'Remove' Barrier (where possible)
Fine Motor	• Provide opportunities for the learner to use alternative means of recording, including typing, voice recording or working with a scribe. • Adapt equipment such as using pencil grips, triangle pencils, writing slopes etc. • Ensure the learner can work with others to contribute verbal ideas.	• Explicitly teach and rehearse vertical, horizontal and circular movements prior to letter formation. • Provide opportunities to rehearse fine motor skills including cutting, drawing, painting, using tweezers, colouring, weaving and threading. • Explicitly rehearse control and movements of fingers following an individualised programme.
Gross Motor	• Use aids or adapt equipment to enable participation. • Adapt the environment reducing risks to the learner or others.	• Explicitly teach and rehearse skills of concern working individually or in small groups. • Follow an individualised learning programme informed by a motor movement audit.
Sensory	• Where appropriate promote the application of senses during learning experiences and encourage learners to 'notice' or if appropriate ensure access to aids. • If necessary modify delivery of information to accommodate sensory needs or preference.	• Explicitly teach and rehearse sensory skills and the independent use of sensory aids. Seek additional advice and training from Specialist Sensory Support Staff to provide a personalised programme.
Mobility	• Adapt equipment or use aids to support movement and where possible to maximise independent movement. • Regularly review tasks to ensure that no learner is 'disadvantaged' or prohibited from participation due to mobility demands of the task. Where necessary adapt, modify or change the task to enable participation and inclusion.	• Where appropriate, implement an individualised physiotherapy or Occupational Therapy programme rehearsing key movements as identified.

Stability & Balance	• Provide aids or support as necessary, including supportive cushions, standing frames etc. • Ensure equality of access to learning tasks by adapting materials or requirements as necessary.	• Explicitly target the development of core muscles following an individualised Physiotherapy or Occupational Therapy programme.
Posture	• Provide opportunities for the learner to move around and vary posture at regular intervals. Create 'breaks' so the learner is able to walk and run between sitting, standing or laying. • Adapt seating to accommodate 'feedback' cushions or to enable seating on a beanbag, peanut ball and provide access to a standing desk.	• Work with the learner to identify 'preferred' posture options that enable attention, focus and concentration. Agree the frequency of posture change and develop a personalised posture plan.
Sensory Processing	• Complete a sensory audit of environments evaluating the sensory demands on learners and make adjustments where possible. • Use strategies for filtering sensory information such as wearing headphones or sunglasses to screen out sounds and sights.	• Explicitly rehearse sensory skills to gain more experience of processing the information such as blowing bubbles, chewing, singing, following lights etc. Similarly, explicitly reduce exposure to excessive sensory information following an individual programme, where possible, informed by a Sensory Integration Therapist.

7 Cs Curriculum – Learning Element	Action to 'Overcome' Barrier	Action to 'Remove' Barrier (where possible)
English – reading, writing, spelling	• Provide opportunities for the learner to work alongside a peer who can act as a reader or scribe. • Provide key word sheets to aid access to spelling. • Ask the learner to identify the correct version of a word from 3 examples, as their spelling 'test.' • Listen to audio books. • Use voice recording and spell checkers.	• Explicitly teach rules and strategies for reading, writing and spelling. Baseline skills and target next small step. Use direct instruction, interleaved learning and rehearse skills little but often. • Teach editing skills, so the learner is encouraged to write own ideas and then edit spelling mistakes. • Provide opportunities to develop and extend vocabulary such as word games, listening to stories and having time to talk.
Maths – number, shape & space	• Provide visual prompts such as cubes, number lines, calculators etc to aid calculation. • Encourage the learner to work alongside a peer who can support and prompt learning as required. • Revise key rules and concepts prior to completion.	• Audit existing skills identifying 'gaps' in knowledge. Explicitly teach skills and develop a 'reference' book to aid independent recall in the future. • Explicitly teach concepts in context and signpost relevance and future application. Where possible, link to learner interests or context.
Science	• Ensure visual prompts and modelled examples of concepts. • Provide vocabulary checklists and structured recording forms. • Check out learner's understanding at the start of an activity by asking them to paraphrase instructions. • Promote collaboration with peers who can offer 'peer support' and model understanding.	• Rehearse key vocabulary and where possible pre-teach key concepts. Explicitly teach relevance and future application, stating "this is useful because…" • Use film clips, websites and or books to help rehearse key concepts and skills.
Art & Music	• Provide opportunities for collaborative learning or participation. • Create a 'safe' and inclusive culture where ideas are encouraged and shared. • Adapt equipment for ease of application and use.	• Explicit teach and rehearse key skills in isolation using a range of medium. • Individually or in small groups look at examples of artwork and or listen to music and discuss views and thoughts.

History & Geography	• Explicitly teach key concepts necessary to aid understanding. Scaffold learning with visual prompts such as timelines and relate to learner's own context or experience. • Pre- teach and rehearse subject specific vocabulary. • Use multimedia to aid understanding and to promote thinking and discussion around specific topics. • Adapt materials and resources, ensuring they are accessible and practical. • Provide opportunities for working alongside others to enable modelling and collaboration. • Promote relevance and practical meaning, perhaps going on visits or providing experiences.
Computing	• Explicitly pre-teach key skills, vocabulary and the use of equipment. • Provide opportunities for rehearsal and application of skills. • Provide opportunities for team or paired working, ensuring the learner is working with a peer who is able to model and support. • Provide visual prompts and verbal guidance to aid application. • Record demonstrations so these can be watched again.
PE & Sport	• Explicitly teach isolated skills prior to application within games. • Coach and or rehearse skills developing greater efficiency, fluency and accuracy. • Watch professional games and identify skills applied. • Adapt equipment and or focus on specific elements of games developing skills. • Provide opportunities for team or paired working. • Use positive rewards and praise to positively reinforce efforts.

Implications for SENCOs and SEN Practitioners

However tempting it may initially be, please do not use these grids in isolation. Yes of course, they are written as a starting point, but add to them and modify the presented ideas. Use the grids to help reinforce the concept of action that overcomes a barrier as distinct from action that seeks to remove the barrier. Where possible, protect professional development time so colleagues can share what works best and explore resources such as the Education Endowment Foundation, the What Works series, the Autism Education Trust Progression Framework and the incredible resources of the Communication Trust. **Actively generate your own evidence base of what works for learners in your school by robustly identifying starting points, defining anticipated impact and then measuring actual impact.**

Ensure that the intervention or action matches the need. The whole point of the 7 Cs Learning Portfolio is to encourage the breadth of assessment and intervention for learners with SEN. It is not sufficient to simply do 'more maths' as 'more maths' is the entitlement of every learner anyway! We must identify *why* maths is a barrier to learning and seek to overcome or remove that barrier (if possible,) so we can see improvements in maths. As you quality-assure the interventions in your school or setting, start with an analysis of relevance and then consider the effectiveness and quality of provision.

SEN intervention really is the other side of the same coin of SEN assessment, which is why the second book in the *Essential SENCO Toolkit* series will explore this in much more detail.

Reflections...

- How useful is it to distinguish between actions that seek to overcome barriers to learning and actions that seek to remove barriers to learning?
- Do our current interventions, adjustments and support predominantly attempt to overcome or remove' barriers to learning?
- Could these intervention sheets be a useful starting point for staff in our school or setting?

References

Autism Education Progression Framework (2019) Autism Education Trust.

Bouncing Back & Coping with Change: Building Emotional & Social Resilience in Young People Aged 9–14 (2016) Tina Rae. Buckingham: Hinton House Publishers.

Life Coaching for Kids: A Practical Manual to Coach Children and Young People to Success, Well-being and Fulfilment (2014) Nikki Giant. London: Jessica Kingsley Publishers.

Sensory Processing 101 (2015) Dayna Abraham, Claire Heffron, Pamela Braley and Lauren Drobnjak. Lla Media.

Talkabout – A Social Communication Skills Package (2016) Alex Kelly. Abingdon: Routledge.

The Education Endowment Foundation Teaching and Learning Toolkit (2020) Available at https://educationendowmentfoundation.org.uk/ (Accessed on 13 September 2020).

Time to Talk – Implementing Outstanding Practice in Speech, Language and Communication (2013) Jean Gross. Abingdon: Routledge.

Working Memory Activities: A Workbook to Stimulate Memory Skills (2014) David Newman. CreateSpace Independent Publishing.

10. Getting started

The wonderful thing about a good book, is it can inspire and motivate action. The frustrating thing about a good book, is it doesn't always suggest how or where to start! However inspired we are by an idea, it is not always easy to transfer the idea from the page into the classroom, which is the purpose of this final chapter. As stated earlier, there are no right or wrong starting points for implementing the 7 Cs Learning Portfolio, so trust yourself if you have already thought of an action that you can take, but if you are not sure how or where to start, keep reading!

Consider what appeals to you about this framework. Is it the language of assessment? Is it because it identifies learner strengths as well as barriers? Is it the simplistic tracker or the assess, plan, do and review recording sheets? Start with your preference.

This model could help you and colleagues to adopt a consistent 'language' of assessment that includes but exceeds curriculum attainment. A starting point could be to simply apply the functional approach and share the 7 Cs booklet with staff and talk about strengths-based approaches. You may even begin by introducing or reminding colleagues of the relevance of identifying barriers to learning and not just pursuing diagnoses. You may introduce the concept of 'overcoming' and/or 'removing' barriers to learning and encourage professional reflection as to the bias of actions in the school or setting.

Alternatively, you may choose to adopt the intermediate approach and trial the 7 Cs language with a small number of learners at SEN Support or indeed just one. As part of their next assess, plan, do and review meeting, you could introduce the 7 Cs Learning Portfolio and ask the learner and their family to identify three strengths and three areas for development. You could then look at the progress tracker descriptors of these areas and agree a 'best fit' starting point, allocating a rating scale for each of these. Together you could consider action that could be taken in school, at home or when the learner is out and about, to support achievement in these areas. You could record the *anticipated* impact of the targeted action and agree when to meet to review the *actual* impact. Or you may decide to adopt the 7 Cs Learning Portfolio user guide and apply the 'extensive' approach whereby some or all of your learners at SEN Support have their own printed version of the user guide, which they will use as their own 'self-evaluation' or learning record for the academic year.

It may be that this framework inspires you to develop your own tracker or language of assessment and achievement, where you use some of the 7 Cs and integrate it with other ideas or resources that you have in the school, thus applying the 'your way' approach. The reality is that the 7 Cs themselves are not a definitive list and you may want to edit this accordingly. You can! It is offered as a starting point for your implementation.

The book itself may have encouraged you to reflect on your approach to SEN assessment and to audit the tools and activities you use. Perhaps you want to find out more about dynamic assessment and wish to trial the facilitation of a 'mediated learning experience' in order to 'watch' how a child is learning? Or perhaps you now want to review your SEN profile to ensure that it really is an SEN profile and, you are also aware of those learners who are Disabled and those with Medical Needs. Perhaps you will complete the Venn diagram to capture a visual presentation of your profile, or complete the SEN, D and MN records? The starting point is yours. Consider completing the Action Planning tool that follows to help identify your first step in this process.

SEN Assessment – Professionals' Action Planning Tool

What I liked about the book:

What resonated the most with me at this time was:

What I would like to do as a result of reading this book:

How could I achieve this?

What barriers may I face?

How can I 'overcome' or 'remove' these barriers?

Who would be interested in working with me on this?

What do I need to do first?

Implications for SENCOs and SEN Practitioners

This is our final implications section in this book, so I wanted to thank you for investing your time with me. I genuinely hope this time has been an investment for you and you are beginning to identify the actions you can take as a result of reading this. The ultimate implication for you is to decide if you want to have a go. If you do, be kind to yourself and stay realistic. Perhaps start with the 'functional' approach to applying the 7 Cs Learning Portfolio, where you just share the idea and concepts. Those colleagues who have already done this (at the piloting phase of development,) consistently reported a positive response from staff. Teachers liked the strengths-based approach and the language of the 7 Cs Learning Portfolio as it makes sense and was easily accessible. Start small but dream big! If there is a positive response and momentum for this type of approach, go for it and **maximise the possibilities!** After all, that is what our 'day jobs' are really all about!

If you have enjoyed this book, I hope you will join me again for the second book in our *Essential SENCO Toolkit* series, where the focus shifts from SEN assessment, to SEN intervention.

Index

Note: Page numbers in **bold** refer to tables.